"I'll never forget the first time I met Gretchen B— Street Fair where I knew she was playing. I don't normally seek out singers or actresses but she I was not going to miss. I saw her on the *Dr. Phil* show and was so taken by her inner strength to stand her ground even when Dr. Phil tried to sway her to give her marriage another chance. I loved her immediately and respected her deeply. Little did I know that we would become as close as sisters and she has helped me through good times and bad. Gretchen is force to be reckoned with. She is love, she is talented and strong. I am so proud to call her my sister and, having written an auto-biography myself, I know the guts it took for her to write this. Now she can add another category to her vast résumé. Hell of a writer!"

—**Cherie Currie**, author of the bestseller *Neon Angel*,
lead singer for The Runaways

"Gretchen's story is a 'must-read' for anyone surviving a marital breakup with anyone, famous or otherwise. I know Gretchen personally and she is one of the kindest, loving, and honest person I know. Surviving Danny with grace and dignity—not many could do. This is NOT a trashy Hollywood tell-all, but rather a glimpse into her side of Danny's story. Loved the book and love Gretchen."

—**Geri Jewell**, actress from *The Facts of Life*

"Gretchen is a woman who is full of tenacity and whose heart feels for everyone around her. She accepts all challenges with a positive attitude, which is reflected in her book. Her unique story pulls you in as she walks you through the gallery of her life experiences. Some of the portraits are beautiful and others are not so pretty, but she values and learns from them all. She's a lovely human being and I'm proud to call her my friend."

—**Allison DuBois**, the inspiration behind the hit television show *Medium*,
television producer, and a *New York Times* bestselling author

"What a fantastic read. I laughed out loud on so many pages…and then on others, all I wanted to do was reach out and give [Gretchen] a hug. I love the truth…the 'no holds barred' of it all. It is light in the heaviest of ways, and I am honored to know and love the writer. I can't wait to read it again!"

—**Marie Currie**, artist, singer, songwriter, and actress

"I love this book and could not put it down. Gretchen Bonaduce is one of the coolest chicks I know. A terrific mother and an even better friend, her life has been fascinating and crazy at the same time. There are many life lessons in her story. To top it off, it is written in a conversational and relatable way."

—**Jackie Kallen**, author of *Hit Me With Your Best Shot*
and *Between the Ropes*

"Here's the thing about Grechen Bonaduce: she's a real person who's lived a surreal life. I watched every minute of *Breaking Bonaduce* when it exploded on to the reality TV scene, and I've never seen a show come close to being as raw or real—before or since. As a reality TV editorial writer and podcast host, I was riveted by Gretchen's account of what went on behind the scenes of filming that show, and the decisions that led her into marrying and eventually divorcing Danny. But Gretchen's memoir isn't just about her marriage; it's about being a woman. She's a child who's lost a parent, a sister, wife, friend, and single mother reinventing herself with every breath she takes. Reading her memoir is like sitting down with a good girlfriend and playing a kick ass game of 'Never Have I Ever'—except in Gretchen's case, she most likely HAS! Warm, funny, vulnerable, and 100 percent relatable in its emotional impact, *Surviving Agent Orange* is a must-read for all of us who are just trying to figure it out, and learning to let go along the way."

—**Erin Martin**, writer and host of
the *Pink Shade With Erin Martin* podcast

"Gretchen proves that all those things we learned when we were little really do work. She's made of "the right stuff." Throw that into a crazy mixture of sex, drugs, rock and roll, and total chaos and you have a fascinating story. I am so glad she is sharing her story with us all. May she inspire others to find their own inner strength. I'm sure that is one of her main reasons for writing this—to help others; because, yes, she really IS that nice!"

—**Susan Olsen**, actress on *The Brady Bunch*

SURVIVING AGENT ORANGE

GRETCHEN BONADUCE
SURVIVING AGENT ORANGE

FOREWORD BY ADRIANNE CURRY

A GENUINE RARE BIRD BOOK

LOS ANGELES, CALIF.

A Rare Bird Book | Rare Bird Books
453 South Spring Street, Suite 302
Los Angeles, CA 90013
rarebirdbooks.com

Set in Minion
Printed in the United States

Photographs courtesy of Gretchen Bonaduce

10 9 8 7 6 5 4 3 2 1

Publisher's Cataloging-in-Publication data
Names: Bonaduce, Gretchen, author. | Curry, Adrianne, 1982–, foreword author.
Title: Surviving Agent Orange: and Other Things I learned from being Thrown under
the Partridge Family bus / Gretchen Bonaduce; foreword by Adrianne Curry.
Description: First Trade Paperback Original Edition | A Genuine Rare Bird Book |
New York, NY; Los Angeles, CA: Rare Bird Books, 2018.
Identifiers: ISBN 9781945572852
Subjects: LCSH Bonaduce, Gretchen. | Bonaduce, Danny. | Entertainers' spouses—
Biography. | Television personalities—United States—Biography. | Reality
television programs—Anecdotes. | BISAC BIOGRAPHY & AUTOBIOGRAPHY /
Entertainment & Performing Arts
Classification: LCC PN1992.4 .B635 2018 | DDC 791.45/028/092—dc23

To Boo Berry and Yung Red

Foreword

By Adrianne Curry

I'D LIKE TO START this intro off by saying this…Gretchen Bonaduce is one of the very few people I can call a friend in Los Angeles. In this cesspool of self-serving filth, she has always been a shining beacon of light to me. I am a very guarded person when it comes to this city, and she has single-handedly torn down every line of defense I've put up to protect my heart. In doing so, she has enriched my experience here and opened my eyes that not everyone who lives here and works in the industry is the spawn of Satan.

I first met her in 2005 at the VH1 Big in '05 awards. I was still with my ex–child star ex, as was she. We were both on hit reality shows and had similar enough backgrounds to hit off some conversation. I immediately knew she was from the Midwest. Her velvety alto voice was a pocket of home I had been missing so much in the beast that is LA. I could tell right off the bat that she was a good person and figured I'd be seeing more of her in the future.

I wasn't wrong. Over the years we have faced many trials and tribulations with each other as guidance. I watched as she left her marriage and struggled to find her own footing after so many stormy years with the father of her children. I witnessed the depth of her kindness when she didn't fight him in court for more than she was being offered (which she would have received if she had asked for it) and marveled at how compassionate she was toward her ex. I saw her tell her children only glowing things about their father, and I appreciated the fact that she tried to keep them out of the whirlwind that was their divorce.

She was there for me during my own divorce. She offered me advice and stood by me as I tried to find my strength I had lost in myself throughout my marriage. During this time, she proved the depth of our friendship by helping me move. As many of you know, very few of your friends will ever be there for you on moving day. I had the pleasure of watching this beautiful, petite woman struggle to lift boxes bigger than her frame and large paintings as I fled my marital estate looking for new beginnings and lost hopes. I was able to return the favor just recently when she rented out her home to a production and had to move into a condo. I busted my ass to return the favor, and I'd do it a thousand more times. That is how much I adore this woman!

I suffer bipolar, and when I feel the sadness overwhelm me and I begin to shut myself off from the world, it is ALWAYS Gretchen who reaches out to me till she breaks my dark mood. This is no easy task as many of you know. Our friendship suffered due to my constant relapses in my depression, but she stuck around. She let me know she loved me and presented me with probably the ONLY thing that could have broken that cycle…she asked me if I loved her as much as she loved me because my distance made her question our friendship. Honestly, I don't think I've fallen that deep in the hole since. She loved me right out of it and presented me with something I didn't realize…my reclusive behavior hurt HER. It didn't help her.

I've watched her daughter blossom into an independent and beautiful woman. I've seen her son bloom in his individuality and tech savvy. I watched as she loved and lost beloved pets, as she navigated the friends who ditch you after your divorce. She has been a part of my life longer than anyone else in Los Angeles, and for this I am eternally grateful.

Through all the bullshit I've seen her go through…crap with her ex-husband, financial struggles, the press…I've never seen this woman stop being kind. Not once. She is such a good person, I feel like a fucking asshole whenever I am with her. If I am grateful for anything from my marriage, it is that I met and befriended the Mother Teresa of Hollywood.

I'm excited for her to tell her story. This is a fascinating woman who has the ability to keep a model with the attention span of a squirrel captivated for almost a decade. This book is a sign of the growth she has gone through her whole life. BRAVO, Gretchen. Give 'em hell!

INTRODUCTION

I'VE BEEN A ROCKER, wife, jailer, television producer, mother, drug widow, and the person who, again and again, put the pieces back together each time my husband shattered our lives. Fortunately, I'm still laughing and creating new adventures at each stage of my life.

My publisher insisted I should have a point to this book. It always annoyed me in high school during required reading that we had to analyze what the author was *secretly* trying to say. It always seemed to me like the author was trying to write a good book that was entertaining and that people wanted to buy. I wasn't sure that every sentence had to be decoded.

But I'll help you out. I haven't set out to make a big point or teach any lessons. There are no secret meanings to unlock—although there may be a lot of things that people wish I'd kept to myself! In other words, I have no secret meaning. If I *had* to make something up, I would say the point is that I do not accept the concept of the long-suffering spouse. I do not admire that quality. At one point I was conditioned to believe that good people stay in their marriages; you work it out no matter what. It seemed kinda cool to be considered the martyr and the saint.

It no longer seems that way. Not at all.

But cut me some slack. The allure of living with a star is strong, and there was a time I could walk into a room and Dennis Rodman would get on his hands and knees and bow down to me, which really did happen at the bar at the Four Seasons. Things like that can totally reinforce staying for the wrong reasons.

(Oh, Dennis Rodman! You always make the wrong choice: Carmen Electra and Kim Jong-un also come to mind.)

Maybe I wasn't the prettiest, the skinniest, or the smartest, but nobody could hang on in a bad marriage like I could. I was an Olympic Gold athlete when it came to that.

So I guess my point is that I got out. And that you can, too, if you need to. It would mean the world to me if you could learn from my mistakes and find the strength within yourself to vacate. (And it's okay with me, too, if you laugh at my expense, in between packing your bags. We'll make it fun and do it together!)

I also want to assure you that this isn't one of those stories about rich people struggling over who gets the silver and who gets the gold. Don't worry—I hate those too! This is the story about a woman who caught some lucky breaks, endured lots of heartaches, and found her own strength in the midst of it all.

Today, as a TV-show producer pitching ideas for new shows, I have to answer the question, "Is it an arcing series?" What they want to know is if, throughout the season, there is a pivotal moment, a catalyst, that will cause change in the characters. Or they want to know if it is a stand-alone series in which each episode has an arc, allowing the show to air in any order.

In that vein, I feel as though my book is the latter.

Have I reached the arc in my life? Looking at my life as a series, I'm not sure. It's hard for me to tell.

Am I at my peak now? Is my peak next week? (If so, I hope it involves sex!)

Was the pinnacle being married to Danny, and was it all downhill from there? No way! My life with Danny Bonaduce opened my eyes and opened some doors for me—while slamming others shut in my face!—and I would never deny that it had some amazing effects on me. But in my life AD (After Danny), I have had my own band, my own TV show, and so many opportunities to express my creativity.

When we first separated, I was pretty sure I would be dead in this town. You know how people say, "you reap what you sow"? What they forget to mention is that this maxim is null and void here in Hollywood, where the more ethical you are, the more you get screwed—and rarely in the good way. One thing I have always tried very hard to do is treat everyone I work with the same, from the caterer to the executive producer. In the past, if I didn't walk in with Danny and people didn't know I was with him, there was a definite difference in how I was treated. I can't tell you how many times some poor makeup artist or equivalent came running after me once they realized that I was the wife of the "famous" guest and gave me an apologetic speech about how "they were so sorry, they didn't realize I was Danny's wife," before magically treating me so much better!

But here's something that may shock you: Nice guys can finish first—even in Hollywood! It used to drive Danny mad that I liked almost everyone. My parents raised me with the saying, "If you can't say something nice, don't say anything," and I've always tried hard to live by that—except maybe in the chapter about one of Danny's ex-radio partners, Janis. (Not her real name, and I'm only human, guys; she was a piece of work.) Danny would often say, "It's not a compliment to anyone that you like them because you like everyone. Is that what you want it to say on your gravestone one day? SHE WAS NICE?"

I've pondered that for quite some time, and yes, Danny, SHE WAS NICE would do just fine.

But I digress. I have been an extremely lucky girl who has had a life far exceeding my wildest dreams. And I want that for each of you. If I were to inspire you in some way to pull out all the stops to get the life you want, that would be the point of my book, too. It takes a lot of hard work. Sometimes the road you think you're going to go down is a beautiful, serene drive through a meadow in the Swiss Alps and it ends up being a wild back-alley ride through the war-torn Gaza Strip. But realize it is the scary Gaza Strip alley that will build your character. The Swiss Alps road is far too easy, and worse, it teaches you nothing.

The lessons are in the hard knocks and the pain. It makes you appreciate the beautiful times so much more.

Jeez, now look what happened. I had no point to this book and now I have twenty!

CHICKEN. IT'S NOT JUST FOR DINNER ANYMORE

March 1991

NOT LONG AFTER I married Danny Bonaduce, I realized all was not well in the Land of Oz. When his drinking would combine with his recreational drug use, he sort of turned into a mental case. Actually, no "sort of" about it. I realized I was going to have to wing this and just do what I had done my whole life: out-tough him. When I was a child, my grandfather gave me the nickname Tough Hobs. I'm not sure where that stubbornness came from, but it would serve me well in my marriage. It was a quality that drove my parents and teachers absolutely crazy. Who knew that that would be the tool that would most come in handy with Danny? I figured my best plan would be to make it impossible for him to get drugs; therefore he couldn't do them. I took away all of his money and gave him only enough for tips or to valet his car. I let him out of my sight only for work purposes, and most of the time when he wasn't on the air, I would tag along. (When he was on the radio, I could hear exactly where he was, so I didn't worry about 5:30 a.m. to 10:30 a.m.)

One night, Danny manufactured some issue to cause a fight, using that as his excuse to storm out of the house. I knew very well what he would do if I didn't stop him: buy drugs and blame it on me. He stormed down the staircase and jumped into his car with me in hot pursuit. Over my dead body would I let him drive out of that garage. I ran outside and threw myself down on the cold driveway and lay behind the tires of the car. I remember looking up at the stars, praying I'd see another day.

"Get out of my way, you crazy bitch!" he screamed as I disappeared from his view. "You'd better move your ass right now."

"NO!" I stubbornly shouted back. "You'll need to run me over before I let you out of this driveway."

He inched the car closer and closer to me.

"Move it, move it, move it," he screamed again.

I wasn't budging. No way in hell was I going to let him get drugs. Not tonight.

Our game of chicken went on for several minutes.

This was God's little joke on me for taking the sanctity of marriage for granted, for getting married only a few hours into knowing each other. I think God misunderstood me. I asked for a challenge, not for the Challenger to blow up in my face.

Danny finally gave up. He threw the car into park, threw the door open, and left the car in the middle of the driveway. He slammed the back door on his way into the house and I lay there a little while longer, thinking about what great news this was for me. I had figured out the line in the sand that Danny would not cross to get drugs: murder.

At least now I knew that. He definitely would not commit murder to get drugs. So I had that going for me. It was the jumping-off point for the longest fulltime job I've ever had: keeping Danny off drugs.

WHY BUY THE JÄGERMEISTER FACTORY WHEN YOU ARE GETTING THE SHOTS FOR FREE?

Summer 1990

I FIRST MET DANNY while living in Phoenix for the second time. I had moved there in 1985 to live with my stepmother and my father, who worked at Palo Verde Nuclear Facility. I drove all the way across the country by myself, which was frightening—and exhilarating. Maybe I sensed the life of adventure that awaited me in Phoenix.

I was so happy when I arrived. It was about 115 degrees and I loved it. The heat alone dropped fifteen pounds of good Southern cooking off my small frame. I quickly found a job at a country club waiting tables and enrolled in Lamson Business College.

Adulthood, here I came—ready or not.

I spent my days going to Lamson and my nights and weekends working at The Lakes Club in Sun City. The work was hard, but I was grateful for the job. I also saw something I have never forgotten: club members who came in all by themselves night after night because there was no one else to care for or about them. The wait staff was their surrogate family.

This was the first time I thought about what it must be like to be old and all alone. I was still young, only nineteen at the time, but I knew I never, ever wanted my life to turn out that way. And even through the most devastating ups and downs, I'm happy to say that I've never felt alone like that. Not even with all the things Danny pulled.

That was then. But my second stay in Phoenix, five years later, and once again living with my parents—it felt pathetic. I felt adrift and totally directionless.

So, when in doubt, party like it's 1999! (It was 1990, nine years too early.)

One night I went to a party with a bunch of friends and decided doing a beer bong looked like a fun idea. One of the seasoned beer bongers showed me the ropes. Punch a hole in your beer, put your lips around the hole, start sucking in and then pull the tab. The beer just wooshes down your throat! Unfortunately, my friend John had failed to warn me to clear the metal pieces so there were no sharp metal edges to cut your lip on. As soon as I pulled the tab, the suction pulled a huge chunk of my lip into two pieces of sharp metal can. Try as I might, I could not pull the can off my lip. I literally sat at a party for two hours with a beer can stuck to my face. I was afraid to go to the ER as I knew I would end up on some medical emergency show about embarrassing injuries.

Thankfully, somehow I was able to get it off. God Lord and I did not want to end up being the pathetic girl that could be counted on to add unintentional entertainment to the party festivities.

I asked God for some clarification, "Why am I here? What am I doing in this town?"

I would soon get my answer.

I found a menial job working as an assistant to a man who owned a production company. It was my job to help him promote whatever events he was doing each week. In October he was producing a psychic fair, and it became my job to get these psychics on radio shows.

Danny was working for the radio station that had what they call a churban (urban, dance, and pop) format. Sadly, they made him go by the name Danny Partridge. I'm convinced that this was a very large part of Danny's drinking problem. To be forced to go by Danny Partridge at thirty-one was extremely humiliating to him.

I was able to book one of the psychics on Danny's radio show. While at the office, I was telling some of the psychics that I was excited to get to meet Danny. A psychic named T Gail told me she had just seen Danny at a haunted house and asked him if she could read his palm.

"I see you are about to get married to a very skinny girl who has a lot of hair," she told him.

"Do you see a name?" Danny asked. That was the exact description of one of the girls that he was dating from the radio station. Unbeknownst to him, this description also fit me!

"Yes, her name is Gretchen," T Gail said.

"I don't know any Gretchens," Danny said as he set up his gig at the haunted house.

When T Gail relayed the story to me, I laughed and laughed. Later Danny told me that the next day, when he picked up his messages and there was a message from me to confirm the psychic on his radio show, he totally freaked out.

When we spoke on the phone, I told him I knew he had just moved to Phoenix and probably didn't know a lot of fun places. I was beginning to appreciate the fact that not only was I back in Phoenix but that I'd been there before and knew places to party. I invited him over to my roommates' house for dinner. (By that point I'd had all I could take at my mom and dad's and was couch surfing from friend to friend.) He showed up with flowers and champagne and wearing a suit with cowboy boots. Cute!

I had labored all day to make a Greek dish called pasticcio. I impressed him right away with my cooking skills, which was good because my roommate Renee (not her real name) was so beautiful she could have been a model. A mean, drunk model, but—still! And at least if he felt he was stuck with the less attractive of the two of us, he knew I could cook. The old saying is true: The way to a man's heart is through his stomach. It also doesn't hurt to withhold sex, but you'll see what I mean soon enough.

DANNY PARTRIDGE MARRIES BLONDE
AFTER 8-HOUR COURTSHIP

[SO SAYETH *STAR* MAGAZINE]

M Y ROOMMATE RENEE, HER date Wade, and Danny and I decided to hit the town, and we were having an absolute blast. I don't remember all the places that we went to—there were copious amounts of Jägermeister and mind erasers being consumed—but we eventually ended up at a place called Chuy's, where the Gin Blossoms happened to be playing. They also became, from that day forward, our unofficial wedding band.

I can't even begin to tell you how the subject of marriage came up. The legend goes that Danny and I got married seven hours into our date, but that's not exactly true. It was hours in, yes, but I can assure you it was more than seven hours. And to make matters more confusing, we both differ on our recollection of who asked whom to get married. Danny says I asked him, but I don't think I would ever have been that bold. I was pretty sure no one wanted to marry me. Me, asking a famous guy? Very unlikely. But if it makes him feel big and macho to think that, fine with me. (Hey, see how easy I am to be married to?)

Danny had just recently gotten out of rehab and was starting to slide back into a bad crack habit again in Phoenix, which goes a long way explaining why he would even contemplate marrying a total stranger. As for me, I had no real long-term plan for my life and this seemed as good of an idea as any. It was one of those Britney Spears moments that at the time just seemed like a funny idea. I don't think I could find a better example as to how much I am a contradiction in terms. I fought for my marriage for eighteen years, yet I would also marry a guy only a few hours after knowing him. Don't worry, it seems weird to me too. And I have no way of making this sound sane, so I won't even try. If this isn't a case for "God works in mysterious ways," I don't know what is. Crack apparently helps, too!

When Danny became a little frisky with me, I informed him, "I can't sleep with *you* unless we are married."

The key word there was "you."

It's not like I hadn't been with other men, but at that point in my life I was not willing to be in a sexual relationship unless I was married to the man.

Why buy the cow when you get the milk for free, right?

Or in this case, why buy the Jägermeister factory when you could get the shots for free?

And sex was the reason Danny wanted to marry me so badly at that point. When you won't let a man have any, he'll do almost anything to get some, including marry you on the first date. We went back to Danny's apartment and pulled out the Yellow Pages. We found a guy named Minister Don and called him. Then we called Renee and Wade to be witnesses.

On November 4, 1990, Minister Don married us. He had no idea that we didn't know each other. Danny was wearing a tank top and jeans, and I was in a red sweater and jeans with the knees ripped out of them. Not exactly the white wedding every girl dreams of. After the ceremony, when it came time to pay the minister, we didn't have enough cash. He had to accept the last seven bucks from a roll of quarters.

We went to 7-Eleven and bought cheap champagne and donuts because we couldn't find a cake. Luckily for me, Renee had thought to bring a camera and was sweet enough to gift the photos to me as a wedding present. Unfortunately, after my marriage to Danny I had to part ways with Renee. Danny said everytime I wasn't around she would tell him that she could take him from me anytime that she wanted, and was constantly putting the moves on him. I certainly didn't need this "frenemy" in my camp. There were enough woman who were not my friends constantly trying to tempt Danny. I didn't need to deal with that in my own home.

That was just the beginning of the crazy twists and turns of life with Danny. He was going to need someone with a steel backbone. I didn't know at the time how strong I was. I was about to go through situations that would have crumbled most people. For instance, a few weeks later, Danny's fiancée called Howard Stern and told Howard that Danny had failed to tell her he had gotten married. Understandably, she was kinda pissed off. (Yes, fiancée, and he'd failed to tell me about her—just in case you're wondering.)

That led to *Star* magazine writing a story headlined, "Danny Partridge Weds Blonde After 8-Hour Courtship."

Danny claimed that his radio station did not want him to disclose that he had gotten married. Maybe. I think secretly Danny didn't want the female listeners to find out. At any rate, nobody, and I mean *nobody*, thought it was going to last.

After Howard Stern and the *Star* magazine article, the cat was out of the metaphorical bag. I always hoped that if his fiancée ever saw our reality show *Breaking Bonaduce* on VH1, she might send me a thank-you card for saving her from all of that nonsense. She did actually contact me via MySpace many years later and said as much.

When we finally told our families, they were about as happy as you might imagine. But you know what? I firmly believe that God works in mysterious ways. I had spent my childhood raised in the Southern Baptist church, and it would be fair to say that most of my decisions were heavily influenced by such a strict and moral upbringing. When I was doing something that I knew would not be condoned by my fellow Baptists, I also knew it wasn't consequence-free. Even if the consequences were just beating myself up in my head for not making the good-girl choice. The problem was 75 percent of me was good Southern Baptist girl and 25 percent was pure party girl. Trying to reconcile the two was difficult sometimes. I wanted to be the good girl, but I also wanted to party like a rock star.

The circumstances of how Danny and I got married are the perfect example of my good-girl/bad-girl thinking. I wanted to have sex, but I also wanted to be married if I was going to have that type of relationship at that point in time. And somehow my brain figured out a way to make it all work out so that, ultimately, I could remain the good girl in the end—at least in *my* head. I also think if we'd not met each other and married, both of us would've amounted to absolutely nothing. That fiery furnace of our marriage changed us in important ways.

Danny was sliding back into drug use and desperately needed someone to slow him down and get him on track. I, on the other hand, was absolutely heading to Nowheresville if I continued down the path that I was on. Maybe best-case scenario, I could've been a singing waitress, but most likely I would've just been a waitress.

Instead, I went on to find out just how strong and creative I am. I knew I wanted to contribute to society in a meaningful and positive way. I feel celebrities have an obligation to do as much good as they can by using their names to support worthy causes. Money and fame boost your ability to help people. I wanted to be a person who would be in a position to help those that deserved and needed it the most, like the people who serve this country and children who are ill or do not have enough to eat. I know as a society we put way too much emphasis on celebrity, but celebrities can earn that respect when they attach their names to a cause. I hoped someday to be in a position where I could be of real use to society.

And Danny would surely either be dead or in jail. He's made that same statement on many TV shows.

So I set about to make an absurd situation with great odds against it into a working marriage.

***

AT FIRST, DANNY AND I settled down into wedded bliss. I was completely enamored by this man's mind. Danny is extremely intelligent. I was impressed by all the things he knew and set about to become his student.

On weekdays, because we had to get to bed so early due to Danny's early-morning radio-host schedule, we'd watch movies. He had a list of movies that he wanted me to watch. I'm sure it was some kind of test to see if I was worthy of him, if I "got" the movies he liked. *Harold and Maude. The In-Laws. The Last of Sheila.* Then it was my turn. *Sid and Nancy, Amadeus, Dangerous Liaisons.* We also enjoyed playing Trivial Pursuit. I won only once. I savored that win and never let him forget that I had beaten him.

A few weeks into our marriage, Danny was invited to be a guest at the '70s Preservation Society party in New York City. That was one great thing about Danny. He loved sharing all the special things he was invited to. It made him happy to take me places I wouldn't ordinarily be able to go.

They flew Danny and me to NYC and put us up at the Chelsea Hotel. Being a huge fan of *Sid and Nancy*, I thought it was cool to stay in the hotel where they spent their last months. That hotel had put up so many fascinating characters: Andy Warhol, Mark Twain, Patti Smith, and Jim Morrison, just to name a few.

That night on Mulberry Street in Little Italy, we met with the two owners of the '70s Preservation Society, Robert Hegyes and Ron Palillo, who starred on *Welcome Back, Kotter*. We regaled them with the story of how we got married. They were sweet and charming, but I'm sure they quietly wondered how long this crazy union would last. Years later, Robert Hegyes wanted me to be part of a web series he was producing. He came to my house to meet with me and sweetly asked me out. Aww. He was the nicest guy, but by then I'd definitely had my fill of ex-child stars. He has since passed away, as has Ron Palillo. I'll never forget how kind they were to me.

The party was at a cool NYC club, which was my introduction to the glitz and glamour in which celebrities live. And we were in the throes of a new relationship, when everyone puts their best foot forward. The beginning of dating is by far the best part; everything seems exciting. Then as time goes on, you eventually decide if you want to make things permanent. And remember, Danny and I did not know each other very well. We got married, then we got to know each other. Danny and I were not only newlyweds but also newly dating, so everything seemed fun. I was loving it!

GREEN-EYED MONSTER MEETS
GREEN-EYED FREE-SPIRIT

ONE THING I HAD to watch out for was Danny learning too much about my past. He was insanely jealous of any man I'd ever looked at—and I'd looked at quite a few! I knew he'd freak out about Bill Hicks, not just because we got along so well, but because Danny would never be the comedian Bill was. Bill, I believe, was our generation's Lenny Bruce.

I met Bill when I lived in Chicago the first time—on my own in 1988. We hit it off immediately, which was a little weird. We were diametrically opposed on many subjects, but even though I might not agree with him, I certainly loved the way he would make his point in such intelligent and hilarious ways. I think he was kind of a frustrated rock star, like myself. We had music in common, and we would play for each other the music that we had written and recorded.

By the time I met Bill, he was on the wagon. Jeez, what is it with me and guys with drinking problems? Of all the things that could be wrong with a man, I tend, for some reason, to attract the drunk ones. Not sure why. Growing up, my Southern Baptist parents (or anyone else in my family) rarely ever drank at all. But over the years, many of the guys have liked were binge drinkers or out-and-out drunks. Playing armchair psychiatrist, I guess it stems from my innate desire to fix people and believing that fixing others would somehow keep me from breaking. Or at the very minimum, keep me from having to fix what was wrong with me.

We spent many lunches and nights at Burton Place, where all the comics would converge after their shows at the Funny Firm, the Improv, and Zanies. I remember the night Chris Farley found out he was going to be a cast member on *Saturday Night Live*. Boy, did he get smashed! Thank God for the bartenders, Tom and Beachboy. They kept me with food and drink in my belly, even when I couldn't afford to pay.

Bill would check in with me from wherever he was on the road. At the time, it didn't occur to me that he really liked me. Years later when I was married to Danny and he was doing *Talk Soup* on the E! Channel, one of the producers walked up to me and told me he'd heard a rumor that I used to date Bill Hicks. I didn't know what to say because a) Danny was insanely envious of Bill's comedic talent, and b) Danny was so insanely jealous. If Danny heard this tidbit of information, he would explode.

I pulled the producer aside.

"Where did you hear that?" I whispered.

"Bill told me," he said.

"Please, please don't say that in front of Danny," I begged him.

He just nodded, and I'm sure he never did. Or else I would have had to pay for that.

I had no idea that Bill had considered our "thing" dating. I was beyond flattered. I am so very honored to be able to say we once dated. And I decided that even if Danny did hear about it, the heat I was going to take would be worth it to claim that I had dated the comic genius Bill Hicks. Bill has since passed. What a loss to the comedy community. Bill was kind of shy when it came to women, I think. He achieved a huge following in England and Australia, but prophets are rarely recognized in their own country. He never achieved here in the States what he did abroad.

Around Danny, I was now pretty used to dodging any questions about *any* guy. It was certainly an exhausting way to live. I wonder if Danny would have been jealous of the first naked man I ever saw. Probably, but that was so crazy, maybe even Danny would give that a pass. I was just a kid, living in Chattanooga then, and…better yet, more on that later.

YOU HAD ME AT BUONGIORNO

In 1987 I met someone I *know* Danny would have been furious if he ever met: Leonardo. He was gorgeous, a composer, and totally cool. From Danny's perspective, what's not to hate?

I met Leonardo through Jeff, a friend in Kenosha, Wisconsin, who wanted to record with me—I had sent him a recording of me singing Bette Midler's "The Rose." Since I had two weeks of vacation coming up at my job at Alamo Rent a Car in Phoenix, and my grandmother lived in Kenosha, I had a place to stay. I flew to O'Hare and had a friend pick me up and take me to Grandma's.

The next day I went to Jeff's home studio, and we got to work writing songs. He had a composer who had already recorded all the music; it just needed lyrics. At this time, Madonna was at the pinnacle of her career so I wanted to emulate what she was doing. I'm pretty sure most of the lyrics I wrote were bad, but I gave it my best shot.

The next day the composer, Leonardo, came in. He was from Italy but had lived in the United States since he was twelve years old and he reminded me of a cross between George Michael and Elvis. That jet-black hair and two-day-old stubble. Jeez, this guy was good-looking, and on top of it he spoke Italian.

I had been in a relationship with a guy named Ryan in Tempe, Arizona, for about two years. Right before I left for Kenosha, I could feel a distance growing between us. I had even found Hallmark cards from another woman addressed to him. The poor guy. I think he wanted to get away from me, but we had intertwined ourselves together by sharing rent on an apartment. Needless to say, the fact that my relationship was on its last legs left me quite vulnerable to a hot Italian guy's charms.

Leonardo and I hung out in the studio all night writing and recording. Mostly we laughed so hard our stomachs hurt. At some point between fits of trying not to pee my pants from laughing, I found out he had a girlfriend who was a flight attendant. All the same, the attraction between us was pretty obvious. So much so that Jed was getting mad at me for falling for Leonardo's adorable shtick. Jed kept warning me that I had better watch out or I could become another notch in this guy's belt. I, of course, insisted that there was no way I could be stupid enough to fall for that.

About ten days into my two-week trip, Leonardo tells me he and his flight attendant girlfriend have broken up. She told him she wanted to get married, and if he didn't, she was going to make her hub in Dallas and move. When he told her he didn't want to marry her, she told him she wanted to break off the relationship.

Game on!

So, go ahead and disregard that paragraph above where I insisted that I could not be swayed by this guy. Apparently I was lying. Soon after, there was some serious hanky-panky going on between us.

I flew back to Phoenix a few days later, and golfer boy broke up with me at the airport. I saw that coming down the pipeline when I heard from him only once the whole time I was gone. I cried a lot, but mostly because I wasn't exactly sure how I was going to pay the rent by myself.

A few weeks later, Leonardo came out to visit me in Phoenix, which was big because he did not like to fly (which is pretty weird since he dated a flight attendant). We had a blast and began contemplating how we could make this long-distance thingy work.

The day he left, I got a call from a girl who said that she was his girlfriend. That part about how he had broken up with his girlfriend? Apparently that was not true. And, to top things off, she and I had been best friends in ninth grade.

Yikes! Ugly situation.

Soooooo, that didn't work out. I hate when guys do that! I'm not the first girl to fall for that "My girlfriend broke up with me" line," and I am sure I won't be the last.

GRETCHEN BONADUCE
ACTRESS EXTRAORDINAIRE...
NOT. EVEN. REMOTELY.

Summer 1991

WELL, AS FATE WOULD have it—or bad fortune, for me—four years later Danny and I were offered a gig in an independent film, *America's Deadliest Home Video*. Why bad fortune? The film was shot in Racine, Wisconsin—the very city where Leonardo lived. Now do you see why I needed to tell you that story? It was a crazy time for us. We were living in Phoenix, and Danny had been arrested. (That little nugget is still to come.) And as if that weren't enough stress, now we would be shooting a film (while waiting for the outcome of his trial) in Leonardo Land! Of all the cities in the whole world, we would be filming in a small town where the likelihood of running into him was high. I pulled over a few of the cast and crew and told them my dilemma. I explained Danny would go totally postal if we ran into Leonardo and the sweethearts promised that they would help run interference, if need be.

One of the hooks that they thought would be great for the movie was to offer me the part as Danny's wife to help create a little extra buzz around the movie. The only problem was I wasn't an actress. I have gone on record many times stating that, in fact, I might be the worst actress in LA. Once when we were filming *Breaking Bonaduce*, the director asked me to walk back out of a building because they didn't get the shot of me coming out. I walked back into the building turned around, waited for my cue, opened the door and walked back out.

As I walked over to the director, he and the whole crew were cracking up.

"What? What's so funny?" I asked.

Between guffaws he said, "That was the most unnatural walking through the door I have ever seen." That was the last time he asked me to do anything over again!

Back on the set of *America's Deadliest Home Video*, I was to play Danny's wife, who was having an affair with Danny's friend (in the film). Part of the direction they gave me for the character was that she was not comfortable being documented on Danny's home movie camera.

Well, I certainly nailed the looking uncomfortable part!

Then there was the issue of being topless, and I was super uncomfortable with that. Plus, because of the nudity and close proximity (i.e., love scene), casting the part of the guy was proving rather difficult. Now that I had warned the production company of Danny's jealousy issues, nobody wanted to take the part!

Finally, a very nice gay gentleman stepped in to play my lover. Danny couldn't possibly want to kick some poor guy's ass who would never be interested in me. It was the perfect solution. I awkwardly did the scene and that was pretty much it for my short-lived acting career.

And, thankfully, I never did run into Leonardo.

Since that time, I have tried to expand my horizons. I have done *The Vagina Monologues* twice and am now cast in a scripted series that is being shopped around. You're never too old to learn, right? I'm just pissed off that at fifty-two I will never get to play the hot girl.Guess it's mom and grandma parts for me!

PLEASE TELL ME THAT IS NOT THE BANJO SOUND FROM DELIVERANCE I AM HEARING

October 1980

I WAS A GREAT wife to Danny. Sure, both parties in any marriage contribute to what goes wrong, but I tried hard to make it work. Eventually, though, I wanted to get back in touch with something I discovered when I was only fifteen years old: I wanted to sing in a band.

In 1980, my dad had accepted a job with the Tennessee Valley Authority (TVA) in Chattanooga. The move from the North to the South was unnerving. I wasn't sure how I would fit into a new high school while looking and sounding so different than the average Chattanoogan—or more appropriately, Hixsonite. My parents found a beautiful house in Hixson in a very nice upper-class neighborhood. I recall the first place we ate lunch, some kind of hoedown place that was probably the predecessor to the Cracker Barrel. As we walked in, I heard these three men sitting at the lunch counter talking about the Civil War. Oh boy, my fear of not fitting in was not at all unfounded.

Luckily, I was able to meet a few of the neighborhood kids before the first day of school. Southern hospitality is no joke. Every day a different neighbor either had us over for dinner or brought us some home-cooked meal.

But my first day at Hixson High was terrifying. Every time I opened my mouth, kids would make fun of me.

"You damn Yankee carpet bagger!"

"Want some pop, you guys?"

Good Lord. Where had I moved? I actually had guys tell me that they wanted to take me out, but their mothers would die if they brought home a Yankee. Most boys in Chattanooga had not seen the likes of me before. I was the first girl to get kicked out of school for wearing a Go Go's miniskirt. I had a bi-level haircut and wore safety pins in my ears. They probably thought to themselves that they could never bring me home to meet their folks, not just because I was a Yankee, but because I looked like a weirdo. One of my favorite things to do was dress as punk rock as I could for church, just to maximize my parents' embarrassment for making me go to church on Sunday.

My parents were not at all amused.

Most of the guys who went out with me were tricked into it by agreeing to go on a double date with one of my friends and her date. Case in point: my senior prom.

My best friend, Rachel, somehow bribed her brother Jeffrey into taking me to dinner, the prom, and the party afterward. I had always heard that a guy expects you to give him some sex on prom night. I was a virgin and this concept was incomprehensible to me. There would be no sex at the end of the evening. So, to ensure that, I was an incredibly rude c-word to my prom date. He opened the car door, and I looked at him and said, "You're not getting sex."

He pulled my chair out at dinner. "Uh, you're not getting sex." Finally, by 9:00 p.m. the poor guy had had enough of me.

"Ummm, don't you have to be home soon?" he asked.

Lucky for him, once we got to the after-party, there were plenty of other people to talk to, so he didn't have to put up with my nonsense anymore. And believe me, if he ever thought he might have wanted to have sex with me, I'd put that to rest forever. At the end of the evening, we all jumped into a pool in our Southern belle dresses. I returned home looking like a drowned rat, but with my virginity still intact.

Fast-forward twenty years: I'm at a Ralph's grocery store in the San Fernando Valley, buying supplies to send to my brother who was serving in the US Army in Iraq. One of the many things on the list was toilet paper, and I had piled my shopping cart to overflowing with as many rolls of TP that it would hold. As I stood in the checkout lane, I heard a voice behind say, "Lady, you okay? That's a lot of toilet paper!" Why how dare this smartass imply, I thought, as I turned around to confront this rude dude. Much to my horror, it was Jonathan! We had quite the laugh over our first and last date.

THE CIA HAS NOTHING ON MY DAD

ONE OF MY FAVORITE establishments—even to this day—was located in downtown Chattanooga. Every week they had a different cover band playing. I was mesmerized the second I stepped through the door. I'd get this excited feeling and I'd hear a voice in my head shouting: "THIS IS WHAT I WANT TO DO!"

I studied the bands that played there: Tom Boy, Cartoons, The White Animals. Trouble was, I wasn't old enough to be in there. One day, as I was sitting at a table totally singing along to the band, the bouncer came up and tapped me on the shoulder.

"Is your name Gretchen?" he asked.

"Uh, like, yeah. Do you know me?" I answered with a huge smile on my face.

"No, but your dad just called and followed you here. He said if we don't kick you out right now, he'll shut us down."

How humiliating. So I was thrown out for a few weeks until I could get my hands on another fake ID. When I finally wormed my way back in, the owner came up to me.

"A little bird told me you're not old enough to be in here," he said. "True?"

I couldn't lie to him.

"Let me tell you something, little missy. We like your business here. You always look so nice. And you don't act like a ho leaving with different guys every night," he said. Little did he know that that wasn't entirely true. I would just make the guy meet me around the corner so no one from the bar would see it. Turns out, the CIA has nothing on me. "You better damn be sure you have that fake ID on you every time you're in my place." Then he let me back in the door.

Soon I found a group that was auditioning singers, and I decided it was time for me to join a band. I was so nervous! I was hoping that their standards would be low. I didn't exactly have Cindy Lauper or Pat Benatar's range, but if they would consider a mediocre singer, I was their girl! Turns out they were, and my dream had come true. No matter that I wasn't the best singer in the world, I would make up for the sound with my enthusiasm and stage presence. Which, by the way, is still my motto. We decided on the name Boy's Life.

I took a day job at Pizza Hut so that I could have my nights off to rehearse and play gigs. Mostly we did obscure cover songs. These guys were so awesome and so much fun. Unfortunately, we were not getting many paying gigs and so the bulk of what I was doing was waiting tables at Pizza Hut. Oh boy. I had to face the reality that if I didn't go to college I was destined to be a Pizza Hut waitress forever. (Please, Pizza Hut…no diss to you, I love your stuffed-crust pizza!)

To make matters worse, the boss at Pizza Hut hated my guts and always gave me the worst jobs, like cleaning under the salad bar on my hands and knees, which obviously had not been cleaned since the seventies. Also, I had to admit, I did not like waiting on all of my peers who were in college. I would try to make my band out to be a much bigger deal so they wouldn't look down on me for being a waitress.

Not long ago, I asked a friend from that time period, Lanell Story, what her thoughts were about me. I wanted to know what people made of me then. Here is what she said:

I met Gretchen in 1984. We were coworkers at a restaurant in Chattanooga and clicked immediately. Gretchen introduced me to enjoying life. I had never been around anyone with such a happy, fun-loving spirit. She was my new, cool, Madonna-dressing friend! We frequented a local bar that had bands playing on the weekends. Her love of a good time and music was apparent the first time we stepped through those doors together. I had never danced standing on a chair before! I don't know if it was because she used to tell me or that I just felt it, but I knew that she was going to be famous someday. Gretchen's friendship will always mean more to me than I can express because when I was going through a confusing time in my life, she was always there to lift my spirits. One particular morning she encouraged me to get out and we went for a ride. As we were driving down a street close to the campus of the local college, there was a truck coming up the street. Gretchen knew the driver and we stopped. The passenger jumped out and as he was going into a house, I thought how silly he looked. We were invited to join them at the lake and my history was forever changed. That silly-looking young man ended up being my husband, so I will always be grateful to Gretchen for going out for a ride with me.

Ha! Even if my mom and dad didn't think so, apparently Lanell and I knew I would be famous. But it would be twenty years before I got in touch with my musical roots again. For now, I had my hands full with Danny—and before long, two kids of my own.

PHOENIX RISING—
AND FALLING HARD

November 1990

A S THE WEEKS WENT on, Danny and I were falling in love with each other. I don't believe in love at first sight. You can't love someone until you actually know them. Lust at first sight, though, that's a different story. That happens every night in every bar in America and around the world.

Ever since I was a little girl I couldn't wait to get married. I wanted to create a stable, loving home like I'd had as a kid—for a while. So I set out to be Susie Homemaker. But I soon realized that there was no way I could keep an actual job. My job was going to be exclusively taking care of Danny.

I would get up and listen to his morning show and clean the house and do the shopping while he was at work. Then, when he got home, I would make a fantastic dinner. (Except once. Apparently, whipped cream and whipping cream are two different things!) Every day he would look at me and say, "There's got to be something wrong with you. I can't find anything wrong with you. How is this possible? Somebody that would marry a guy on the first date has to be batshit crazy."

But I wasn't. We were happy. Then.

A little over a month after Minister Don had married us, we went to the courthouse and filed legally to get our marriage license. After we had the paperwork in our hands, we sat on the courthouse steps and ate hot dogs from a street vendor. Life looked good. We agreed we were in it for the long haul. Danny went to a vintage jewelry store in Scottsdale and bought me an antique emerald wedding ring. It was the most beautiful ring I'd ever seen.

I was determined to show everyone that they were wrong, that we were going to make it. Since I was the only girl in my family, my father and stepmother wanted us to have a real wedding. We started planning a very small ceremony with a sit-down dinner at the Crescent Hotel in Phoenix, and we set the date for May 4, 1991. I wanted to have a buffet so that I could invite more people, but my dad was having none of it. I found a beautiful Christian Lacroix dress and pretty veil all for three hundred bucks.

Meanwhile, though, I started to realize something wasn't quite right with Danny. He began chewing on the side of his mouth strangely. I also started seeing pieces of aluminum foil around. I put two and two together and figured out he was doing some kind of drugs. I'm no Sherlock Holmes, but the evidence was pretty obvious.

I started taking all of his money away from him so that he wouldn't be able to buy any drugs—I gave him only ten dollars each morning to pay for parking. I took his money cards and any access to larger sums of money. He had been pretty much living paycheck to paycheck and had no savings or investments. I was determined to change that.

So, to all of you who love to call me a gold digger, you need to understand that Danny had no money. (You can go ahead and kiss my heinie now!) Danny trusted me to make the right choice about our finances. That was pretty amazing because he didn't know me, but he correctly sensed that that I knew better than he did.

We were living in downtown Phoenix, and at that time, it wasn't a safe place to live, so we decided to adopt a dog from the Great Dane Rescue Society. We brought home Max, and he became the third Bonaduce.

He affectionately became known as Maxi Priest.

Max was great with us, but he hated other dogs. Once, when Danny was doing stand-up in Buffalo, New York, we took Max with us. It was the dead of winter and there was a lot of snow and ice on the ground. Max and I went out the door, and almost immediately Max saw another dog across the busy street and took off running. I tried to throw myself on the ground to stop him, but all that did was turn me into a dog sled. Max tore across the parking lot toward the street dragging me behind him. I didn't even think about letting go, because I was afraid he would get hit by a car. Anyone looking out the hotel window must have had quite the laugh at this gigantic dog dragging a girl across the snow and ice.

The weekends were always extra challenging with Danny. Since he didn't have to be up early for work on Saturday and Sunday, he wanted to stay out all night long. I hoped he would drink just enough to pass out for the night. I didn't want him waking up in the middle of the night wandering off to buy drugs.

I started hiding the keys in the washing machine so if he woke up he wouldn't be able to drive off. I slept with my hand on him so if he moved I would wake up. He had a clause in his contract that they could randomly drug test him at any time and after one particularly trying weekend, Danny told me he had something important he needed to ask me: Could I pee in a cup so he could sneak it into the clinic?

He had gotten ahold of drugs and knew he would not pass a random drug test. He had also figured out a system where he could bring in other people's urine and use the sink to heat the sample to body temperature, and he began sneaking in little throwaway thermometers that he smuggled in his jean pocket.

I was furious. I didn't like being put into a position to lie, and it wouldn't be the last time that I would be in that position for Danny, as it turned out. A dirty urine sample would certainly cost him his job, which meant we'd both be ruined. I would help dig him out this once.

Good thing they didn't test it for female hormones!

Did he learn his lesson?

Why, no.

Danny tells a story in his book, *Random Acts of Badness*, about how he talked the guy administering the test into peeing for him once too. That's the thing—people felt sorry for little Danny Partridge. I think people, including myself, did him a terrible disservice as a human being. He never had to face the consequences for his behavior. Because he was so charming and people felt so bad for him, there would always be someone to bail him out of trouble. And that included me, of course. Which gave him carte blanche to continue to act like a jackass.

Which he did in spades—right before our wedding.

WHAM, BAM,
NO THANK YOU, MA'AM

January 1991

A TV STATION IN Phoenix had given Danny a shot at a show. Danny and I wrote, directed, and filmed an entire episode. Pretty awesome for people who had no idea how to work cameras and run sound.

The last night of filming, Danny and I decided to throw a wrap party for all the people that had helped us out on the show. We went to some pizza place and treated the cast and crew. We were a loud and raucous bunch. Especially me. I was so relieved to have this over with, as half of the time Danny had just been screaming at me about this or that.

It was the Saturday before Easter Sunday.

When Danny and I got home, we decided to have a little nightcap. Danny handed me my usual screwdriver. I took a few sips and became very sleepy. It was getting late. I fell asleep for a little while and woke up a few hours later.

Danny was nowhere to be found, and I had a very, very bad feeling.

I grabbed Max and walked around the neighborhood trying to find him. I went to the 7-Eleven. I asked if they had seen him. They lied, said no.

I walked to the Arizona Center and asked the people at Fat Tuesdays if they had seen him. They said no.

I was starting to panic. I walked back to our condo and heard a bunch of cars racing by. What on earth? Then a helicopter flew overhead. I entered my apartment through the back door and heard furious knocking on my front door.

When I opened it, at least twenty cops were standing there.

"Ma'am, a guy just raped a woman and ran into your house," a cop yelled at me. This is untrue, but at the time that was their impression.

"Oh my God!" I screamed. "Come in."

Ten officers flew by me. I had no idea what was going on, but I was frightened that an intruder had run into our place. A minute or two goes by, and then there's an awful commotion. The police officers were at the top of the stars, dragging Danny down the steps—naked. That's right, I said naked. And you have to remember at this point they think he has attacked a woman, and they're treating him accordingly.

When Danny got home he had taken his clothes off and jumped into the bed. He'd wanted them to believe he had been at home sleeping all night. But then when he heard them coming, I guess he got so scared that he jumped in the closet, which was where they found him.

They handcuffed me and took me outside, all the while Danny kept yelling, "Tell them I was home all night. Tell them I was home all night."

They took me outside the gate and asked me to identify our car. Now, I'd seen *Miami Vice* enough times to know not to say a word. I told the cop I wasn't going to say anything until I had a lawyer, which infuriated him. They put me in the back of the police car and left me for what seemed like hours. Finally, they took me outside the condo to find out what I knew: which was nothing.

In their effort to try to get me to incriminate Danny, they started saying things I just could not comprehend. But eventually they left, taking Danny with them on their way. They did let him put on shorts, however. My shorts. Teeny tinny little shorts. Served him right!

To say I was hysterical would be an understatement. First, I called my parents. Next, I made a call to his sister in Los Angeles, because I did not want to call Danny's mom and tell her this news. Then I lay down in a fetal position and began to cry. My Southern Baptist parents, who were gearing up for Easter Sunday, came rushing over to my rescue.

Sometime in the early morning, I got a collect call from jail.

And you bet I wanted an explanation. What could he say? I know he sat in the jail cell trying like hell to come up with some explanation that people would understand—especially me.

It was Easter Sunday and all of the banks were closed for the day. I found a bail bondsman that would let my dad put up his antique cars to get Danny out—if that doesn't right there tell you how wonderful my father is, nothing ever will—and I picked Danny up from jail. He came walking out in my little shorts, no shirt, and a patch over his eye.

Now, I *cannot* believe they didn't drug test him. Or if they did, I don't know how in the world Danny got around it. I knew he had to have been on something, but the best I could get out of him was this: He was giving this girl a ride home and realized there had been a big misunderstanding. Namely that the girl was a trans woman. Danny said that once he realized she was trans, he told her to get out of the car. But she wanted money and a fight ensued. Unlucky for Danny, a cop car was parked around the corner, and when he heard the fight he turned on his lights. Realizing that "Danny Partridge Caught with Prostitute" would be the morning headline, he decided to flee the cops in a high-speed chase.

Jesus, Danny.

I wanted to strangle him at this point. His story was probably bullshit, but I wanted to believe him. Months later a fellow DJ, Jonathan Brandmeir from the WLUP in Chicago, interviewed Danny and looped together all the many versions of the story he had told. Depending on who Danny was talking to, he'd spin the version he thought would work best. The Oprah version (bullshit sanitized version), the Howard Stern version (probably closest to the truth), the Katie Couric version, and so on.

Sure enough, when we get home from bailing him out of jail, we turn on the TV. Top story.

If anyone had a right to cut and run at that point it would have surely been me. But I decided that I'd said, "for better or worse," and this was certainly worse now, wasn't it?

Sometimes religion can victimize you. You are so conditioned to keep your marriage together that you put up with things you shouldn't for the sake of being a good Christian. I thought it was a badge of honor to be the long-suffering wife.

Of course, that's a load of crap, and I hope more and more women know this now. Back in 1991, things were different. We *knew* we needed to do things differently, but changes to such deeply rooted habits take decades to evolve. But even back then, Danny knew he had gone too far and invited me to vacate with his blessing. He had embarrassed himself, me, his family, my family, his work. Christ, this was horrifying.

I was so not prepared for this. Not only was it the top story on the local news, but now reporters had begun knocking on our door. It had hit the national news. *Entertainment Tonight*, *Hard Copy*, all the tabloid shows. "Danny and the prostitute" was the story of the day.

In between fielding mean calls from DJs—Danny being in radio meant most of them had our number, and DJs are the meanest lot there is!—I found an attorney named Richard Gierloff, who was willing to take the case and hire a PI to investigate the trans woman. This was going to cost a fortune!

Danny was still on probation in Florida from a wonderful bust there, where he was caught trying to buy drugs. The special irony being that he was in town that week to host a "just say no to drugs" event for MTV.

Now, one of the charges he was facing was reckless endangerment stemming from the high-speed police chase. Do you know the penalty for reckless endangerment while on probation in Arizona? Oh, that would be life if convicted!

And to top it off, Danny was fired from his radio job. Suddenly, we were going to have to get very creative on how to make a living.

IT WAS HARD TO GET COLD FEET
IN 112 DEGREES

May 1991

WITH DANNY'S ARREST AND all his other troubles, our finances were shot. But luck was on our side for once—in a peculiar sort of way. The nineties was the era of the ex-child star gone wrong: Dana Plato had recently tried to rob a video store, Todd Bridges was accused of shooting someone, and Danny Partridge had a date with a hooker.

All the TV hosts did ex-child-star-gone-wrong shows, including Oprah. And lucky for us, Danny was AFTRA, so they would have to pay an appearance fee.

Bingo. Income.

But first, we still had the matter of our wedding to deal with. It was too late to cancel it, my dad had put too much money down, and people had bought plane tickets to come in to attend our nuptials. My parents had already paid every cent they could and I did not want to ask them for more money. I tried desperately to figure out what we could cut back on. One thing we definitely could not afford was a photographer. Without telling my parents, I made a deal with *Star* magazine—in exchange for exclusive rights to the wedding, they would give me copies of the wedding pictures.

The day before the wedding, pretty much everyone had shown up. Danny's family from LA, his groomsman, my bridesmaids from Chicago and Tennessee, and my sister from Seattle.

My family was tapped out, as was Danny's mother, who put up the retainer for the attorney. We couldn't afford to have a proper rehearsal dinner at a restaurant, so we had it at my parents' house.

The morning of my wedding, I woke up early. But there was no need to hurry. Hair and makeup wasn't standing by to make sure I looked more beautiful than I ever had for my big day—there was no money for that.

I met up with everyone at the Crescent Hotel; at least we were able to afford a room to get ready in and to stay in for our honeymoon night. The bridesmaids and I got ready together in my room, and it was so great to have some of my friends to rally around us for our day. Most of them didn't have great jobs but still managed to pull enough cash together to come and pay for bridesmaid dresses.

Meanwhile, Danny being Danny, he thought it would be a fantastic idea to spend the day getting lit at Hooters.

When the hour arrived for the ceremony, I took one last look in the mirror. In every girl's imagination, her wedding day is the happiest day of her life. Glancing at the girl in the mirror, I looked deep into her eyes and knew that this was not in fact the happiest day of my life. All the same, I put on a brave face and walked down the aisle with my amazing dad. I wondered if he felt the same way. Isn't it supposed to be every dad's dream to walk his daughter down the aisle to a loving husband who will cherish and love her forever?

Minister Don came down to marry us again, and it was a beautiful ceremony on a gorgeous hot day in Phoenix. Everyone sat down and dinner was served. Half of my wedding party had disappeared. I was furious when they didn't come down to eat. I would have invited more people had I known they were just going to be upstairs doing cocaine instead of eating dinner.

We could not afford a DJ or a band; lucky for us, a lot of the people at the wedding were musicians so it turned into a big jam session. Finally, something great at my wedding!

To top off the glorious day, *Star* magazine sent me only seven pictures. My parents were furious when they found out I had made a deal with the devil. I did like the picture they printed in the magazine, though. So at least there's that.

The next morning it was back to worrying and trying to figure out our future, what with the terrible problems looming on the horizon. I wasn't sure things could get any worse.

Oh, but they did.

I DO NOT TRUST A GENERATION THAT WOULD LET "MUSKRAT LOVE" REACH #4 ON THE BILLBOARD CHARTS

('CEPT YOU, MOM. YOU WERE DEAD. YOU'RE EXCUSED)

My parents, Thomas Hillmer and Mary Belisle, were teenage sweethearts. They lived a block away from each other in Zion, Illinois. They started dating when my mother was a freshman at Holy Child Catholic girls' school and my dad was a junior at Zion Benton High School.

From what I understand, my grandfather, Vincent Belisle, was a very strict Catholic and a very serious man to boot. His wife—my grandmother, Harriet Lauritzen—had died while giving birth to my aunt Katie in the 1950s. People say that this devastated my grandfather, that he never fully recovered. I don't know if it was just pure, good old-fashioned depression or if maybe he had been bipolar or schizophrenic. I think at that time, people were less likely to throw out all kinds of diagnoses as they do today.

My mother had attended Catholic school her whole life until she fell in love and begged to attend the same school as the object of her affections.

The year was 1963, and against his better judgment, I'm sure, Grandpa Vince relented—and rued the day of that decision.

That same year, my mother got knocked up and nine months later gave birth to my older brother Kurt. Yikes! This was the sixties, and though times were changing, this was still a very big no-no. In 1963, if you were Catholic and pregnant *and* sixteen, you got married. That was that.

My mom and dad told my father's mother, Marguerite, who then walked down the block to the Belisle residence, and together they told Grandpa Vince, who I'm sure you can imagine was less than thrilled. In fact, I think it would be fair to say that Grandpa Vince—oh, let's not put too fine of a point on it— hated my father!

And so my dad moved into my grandfather's house after he and my mother were married, where he received quite the chilly reception. Most verbal correspondence between my father and grandfather was done through my mother. When they sat together at the table eating dinner, my grandfather would look at my mother and say, "Tell Tom this," or "Tell Tom that," even though my dad was sitting right there and could hear him perfectly.

My dad's parents insisted that my dad finish high school, and so he attended classes during the day and worked at Abbot Labs after school. Hard, hard life when you are teenage parents.

On July 13, 1964, my brother Kurt was born. And then fourteen months later I came along. Because what could be more joyous than being teenage parents to one kid in diapers when you could go ahead and have two?

My mother preceded the MTV show *16 and Pregnant*. She saw the trend years before it happened and jumped on board. That's how cool my mom was!

By all accounts, my mother was quite the elitist. She was a rather snooty girl, which was funny because she came from middle-class stock. No reason to have airs about her, but she did. She adored Jackie O and patterned herself after her. Even in their wedding photos, my mother was wearing a very smart suit and hat. I see where I get my love of big hair, hats, and giant sunglasses.

My parents tried so hard to be happy in their circumstances, but how could they? They had two small children and very few friends—a number that quickly dwindled, as they were more interested in having fun, graduating, and going away to college. Not to mention the uncomfortable situation at home between my dad and grandfather.

I can't imagine.

Ultimately, by 1969, they realized that if they had any chance at all of being happy, they would need to get out of the toxic environment they were in and get their own place. One of the only times that my grandfather actually spoke directly to my father was when my dad informed Vince that he and my mother were moving. Weird how he could not stand my dad but was not particularly happy that we would be leaving his home. It seems as though it would have been a relief to him not to have to deal anymore with a guy he didn't like and two screaming kids.

Dad said Grandpa Vince started pacing and just kept asking my dad over and over,

"So, you're really moving out?"

"Yes, Vince. Mary and I and the kids are going to get our own place."

"Really? You're moving out?" Grandpa asked again.

"Yes, we are." Then my father left for work.

A few hours later, Kurt and I came home from school to find an ambulance in front of our house. My mother sat on the front porch crying and wouldn't let us go inside. We sat beside her as she explained that our grandfather had fallen down the stairs and had a heart attack and died.

It was my first experience with death and remains quite vivid in my mind. I wasn't sure how to process it. Years later I would learn that he had actually hanged himself in the basement of our house, and my mother and aunt had found him.

How sad. I had always heard that he never recovered from the death of my Grandma Harriet, and maybe one more loss was just too much for him to take.

A D-MINUS *MINUS* IS AN ACTUAL GRADE IN MY BOOK

I don't think I could have asked for a more stable upbringing. My parents were very, very strict, that part I hated. I spent many nights grounded from TV, the phone, and hanging out with my friends. I was not particularly interested in school and just wanted to be a social butterfly. My grades left something to be desired. I only got away with murder at school because the teachers liked me.

I remember one of them gave me a D--. That's right, a D-minus *minus*. My mother had a real problem with that. She said a D-minus *minus* is an F. Fail her! My social studies teacher told her he liked me too much to fail me. I did have an uncanny ability to be a teacher's pet, even if I wasn't the best student.

The only time I cared was in eighth grade when I wanted to try out for the cheerleading squad, and you had to have at least a C average to join. I busted my rear to bring up my GPA so I could be eligible. I tried out and got on the squad. Not only that, I got to be captain! The icing on the cake was that because I was the smallest, I got to be at the top of the pyramid. Being totally scrawny was going to pay off. After years of torture from the boys that I had no boobs or butt, my reward would be to get to be "on-top pyramid girl." You can see how my goals in life were quite high.

My life was complete. I spent my days practicing cheerleading, babysitting for extra money, and smoking pot with my friends. Luckily, I got my drug use out early. Bad grades, smoked some pot, smart mouth. That was the extent of my badness. Maybe that sounds bad to you, but at least I wasn't knocked up, a serial killer, or most wanted by the FBI. (Or wanted by them at all, actually.)

On the weekends I worked as a candy striper at Saint Catharine's hospital, one of my favorite jobs of all time! Sometimes I would deliver flowers or blood or clean up all the mess after a disaster drill. By far the best job of all was working in X-ray, mostly because I loved the two X-ray technicians so much they would send me to pick up patients and assist during the X-ray process. I tried to find reasons to go to the alcoholic ward. There was a cute guy in there who played The Cars record over and over. My first obsession with an alcoholic man and cool musical groups! My future was making itself heard already.

***

September 1969

THE FIRST TIME I ever encountered the name Danny Bonaduce was in the fall of 1969. We'd returned from Phoenix, after the summer of divorce, to Zion, Illinois, where my mother had moved back into the house we lived in with my grandfather. That must have been hard on her.

We moved into the upstairs apartment. My brother and I shared the only bedroom, and my mother slept on a foldout couch in the living room. Kurt and I would wait for her to fall asleep, and then we would sneak out and watch TV under the sofa bed right underneath her while she slept. This is one of the only memories I have of watching the *Partridge Family*. I vividly recall watching the opening credits and trying to figure out how to pronounce Danny Bonaduce's last name. I could never have imagined that one day I would share that name.

My mother worked as a keypunch at Fort Sheridan, outside of Chicago. Early every morning, she carried Kurt and me to the car and drove us to the babysitter's in the dark, where we stayed until we had to go to school. Then she would pick us up after her day was over. Mother came from a very close family, and on the weekends my dad didn't have us, we spent time at my aunts' houses with all our relatives. There was usually a big party. I remember those days so fondly.

***

AFTER THEY SEPARATED, MY father and mother found new partners within a year or two. I don't think either of them were cut out to be alone. In my dad's case, he met my stepmother, Wanda, at a college hangout nightclub called the Lighthouse in Kenosha, Wisconsin. I'd lay money it was probably one of the few times Wanda was ever in a bar. God does work in mysterious ways! She turned out to be the love of my father's life and as I sit and write this book they have been married for over forty years. (That's like one hundred and twenty Hollywood years!)

As I recall, they met and married within eight months of knowing each other. It seems us Hillmers *love* to get married quickly, though I'm not sure her parents were too excited to have their daughter marrying a divorcee with two small children.

My mother on the other hand, found a military man named Rex, who was a sergeant in the army and whom she eventually married. I remember him being a very quiet guy, and I believe my mother was very happy with him.

Soon after they married, Rex received orders that he would be stationed in Germany. I know my mother was very excited about living in Europe. She was finally living her Jackie O fantasy of being a well-traveled woman of the world.

A BIRD IN THE HAND IS WORTH
TWO IN THE STOCKERBUSH

O_{N THE OTHER HAND}, this move did not sit well with our father. He would get to see his children maybe once a year. I didn't think too much about not being able to see my dad. I was wrapped up in the excitement of moving to Europe, which would be the beginning of my intense love affair with Europe. We packed up our place and relocated to Buren, Germany.

My stepfather was stationed at a NATO outpost that was also shared with the Belgian military. When we first arrived, they did not have housing for us, so we spent several weeks in a German hotel.

I loved it! I slept in the crib in the room so my brother could have the bed. My mom and Rex had the other bed. I thought it was funny to sleep in a crib, as I was seven years old at the time! It had the thickest down comforter and I felt like I was sleeping on a cloud. Under any other circumstances, I would not have been allowed to sleep in a crib.

My mother had talked the hotel restaurant into making Kurt and me lunch every day to take to school. I can still taste the German bread they used to make our ham and butter sandwiches.

My mother was eager for us to experience the local cuisine. One night in the restaurant, she made me try the wiener schnitzel. It tasted like gristle. Gross! I hated it! My mother said I had better swallow it, or else. I sat with that gristle in my mouth for five hours and could not get up from the table until I did.

"You swallow that piece of meat!" Mom said.

"NO! I hate it!"

"You will sit there in that spot until you do!"

Another testament to my stubbornness and, as I like to call it, my "I will out-tough you" approach to life: I finally thought I could get away with spitting it in the toilet, but I got caught. Boy, was she mad! To this day I will never make my kids swallow something they don't like. *Hmmppf.* I showed her, now didn't I?

But when I think about it now, I realize that we both lost five hours of our precious life together that we could never get back. What I wouldn't give to have those five hours back with my mother. I would swallow a hundred pounds of gristle to have her back again.

Not long after that contentious situation, I learned the reason for her recent edginess: I was going to have to vacate the baby crib as an actual baby was going to be needing it.

Now, the hotel would no longer do for our family.

My mother wanted to have her own home and not bring our new sibling to live in a hotel. I think my stepfather put the pressure on the Army to find us a place to live. Finally, we were settled into a little two-bedroom apartment in military housing, although it was on the third story. No doubt that was not easy for a pregnant woman hauling groceries and laundry, but at least it was a home for her family.

Kurt and I went to the American school on the base. We did not have an easy time of it all. The kids picked on us, and many days we came home from school after being in fights.

Nothing like being a military brat to toughen up the softest kid. It forces you to learn to adapt to new places and people no matter how hard the challenge. Not that I was a soft kid in the first place, but I think my brother Kurt was much more sensitive. At least half of my fights were in defense of my big brother. Kurt and I fought like cats and dogs, but oh the fool that wanted to be mean to Kurt. They had me to contend with, and I would not back down from a fight when it came to defending Kurty.

I don't think my mother had an easy time making friends, either. If she hadn't been so happy with my stepdad and the new baby on the way, things would have been much more difficult. I recall she was sick almost the whole time she was pregnant. She loved to eat noodles, with milk and sugar—not sure if it was a pregnancy craving or a Danish thing (my mother's mother was 100 percent Danish). My mother's grandparents on her mother's side were full Danes. They ate a lot of strange things.

In April, my little sister Aimee was born. I can't remember going to see my mother or new baby sister at the hospital, but I may have. I hope I did because within days, my mother was dead from childbirth complications. That changed my life so dramatically—not only were we on the move again, but it would leave its mark on why I tried so hard to make my marriage work. I wanted my children to grow up in a safe, stable, and loving family.

My dad and his wife Wanda offered to adopt Aimee so that we could all stay together. Because Rex was in the military he wasn't exactly equipped to take care of a newborn. Rex declined, and his twin brother and sister-in-law took her back to Seattle where he was from instead. I think it would have been better for all of us to stay together, but that was the way it worked out.

After my mother's funeral, we headed back to live with our parents. That term now means only our dad and stepmother, Wanda, who lived in Kenosha, Wisconsin. We really were the Cleavers. Church on Sunday, dinner at five o'clock sharp consisting of meat, starch, milk, vegetables, and—of course—dessert.

My dad was happy to have his children back with him. I hardly ever saw Aimee growing up, but my parents made a concerted effort to be sure we stayed in contact. When she was eighteen, Danny and I moved her out to Chicago and helped her get a job at Planet Hollywood. She lived in Chicago for about a year and then went back home to Seattle. After she moved, I didn't know where she was, and we didn't have much contact. Thank God for Facebook, or I still wouldn't know where she'd gone.

I CHILLED ON SILK SOFAS, CHATTING WITH OPRAH

[THANK YOU WILL SMITH FOR
WRITING SUCH A PROFOUND SONG!]

June 1991

PEOPLE TEND TO BECOME a lot nicer when they're under indictment. While we waited for Danny's court date, we spent most of our time sitting around the house because it was too embarrassing to go anywhere in Phoenix.

Danny spent a lot of time writing an article that he eventually sold to *Esquire* magazine. He was such a great and funny writer. It could have been a second career choice, had he wanted to go into journalism. If nothing else, it was a productive way for Danny to pass the time. He wasn't allowed to leave the state unless we had written permission and clearance from the State of Arizona. When he was offered a job of some kind, we would ask, and usually they would let us.

Every once in a while he would have a court date and we would have to go down to the courthouse with Richard Gerleiff, our attorney. Having seen footage of us walking hand in hand in court, I couldn't look more like a deer caught in the headlights. He'd had years of practice of being in the spotlight; I had weeks. And for my newfound fame to be for my husband's chick-with-dick problem—I can't think of a more embarrassing reason. Thank God it was 1991 and every single thing happening wasn't being documented online!

My first foray into TV happened to be *The Oprah Winfrey Show* in Chicago. As I mentioned before, she was one of the daytime TV shows that did the ex-child-star-gone-wrong episode. I don't think I could ever explain to you how nervous I was. To be on national TV, with Oprah… I knew she was not going to be easy on us.

Before the taping, someone brought us back to be introduced to her. She could not have been more of a sweetheart, grabbing my hand and taking me with her as she walked around giving last-minute instructions to her crew, all with me in tow to put me at ease.

I was less than impressive on her show. I called myself a five-hundred-pound dress or something that made absolutely no sense out of my nervousness. My biggest memory from that day: I recall these two jackass DJs in the audience implied I had married Danny for his money and fame. He didn't have any money and the fame he had was quickly devolving into infamy. Typical DJs trying to get attention by doing something outrageous. Well, at least my old Chicago roommates were in the audience and tried to stick up for me. It's a day I will never forget, as much as I would like to! I'm sure if this book does well enough I will be on shows where they will happily find the footage to embarrass the shit out of me. Can't wait!

Around that time, some real financial help came in the form of David Cassidy, who was going out on a small United States tour. He offered Danny the opening slot. Danny would be doing standup on some of his dates.

While we waited for the final court date to see if Danny was going to have to spend some time in jail, Danny's old Philadelphia radio station, Eagle 106, was miraculously interested in rehiring Danny. They had fired him a year or two before for drinking on the air. I think they had had enough of him after he was arrested in Florida for the drug arrest while employed by them. To their credit, they were also the company that put him into rehab for the first time.

I did not want to let Danny out of my sight, but if he got the Philly job, I was going to have to get us moved to the other side of the country. I also suspect he didn't necessarily want me out there, what with having a wife cutting into time he'd otherwise devote to picking up chicks.

This guy was going to be a very tough nut to crack.

When he came back from the tour, I unpacked his bag and found jewelry that wasn't mine. Now, I think after a wife has stayed with her husband through this period, he would owe her for the rest of their lives. But oh no. Not Danny. He had already begun to slide back into his old ways.

Now, I know what you're saying. Why did you stay? I couldn't prove it. And I wasn't willing to walk away from my marriage over something I thought was happening but could not prove. You will probably want to ask me that many, many times while you read this. I don't know the answer to all that. I guess in a way my life had a purpose.

I have realized that many of the people, male and female, that I have attracted into my life have been broken people. I'm a fixer. This was the ultimate fixer-upper.

Danny had such tremendous potential to be an incredible human being. He was so very smart, talented, funny, and had a gigantic heart. He was also the most broken man I have ever known.

When our last court date came up, we were scared. We had heard Danny was going to get sixty days in jail, but our attorney gave such a great closing argument that the judge changed his mind on the bench and gave Danny a ninety-day suspended sentence. We were elated that he would not be going to jail. More good news would soon follow, too: Danny got the job back in Philly!

Moving around so much as a kid would serve me very well as a grown-up. I had moved and lived so many places that every time Danny got transferred to a new city, I didn't mind at all. Some people become attached to their surroundings and find it hard to move around. I have never felt that way.

So we packed up Danny's Camaro. Danny, me, and Maxi Priest drove across country to Danny's Aunt Jackie's house. We were now $30,000 in debt and couldn't afford our own place, but we were happy. We were heading into a new adventure.

CITY OF BROTHERLY LOVE—
OR SO WE THOUGHT

January 1992

W<small>E LIVED WITH</small> D<small>ANNY</small>'s mother and Aunt Jackie at first. It would take us a while to dig out from the legal bills that we had acquired from Danny's "hilarious" prostitute beatdown. Danny's family was incredibly kind to put up two heavy smokers in their beautiful home. Philadelphia was such a lovely city! I was apprehensive to be moving to a city where I suspected Danny's drug problem was probably at its worst. He knew every bad corner, every dangerous project location to purchase drugs.

I certainly would need to be on my toes to keep him out of trouble here.

Danny was back on Eagle 106 with a morning show called "John Lander and the Nut Hut." John was an elder statesman in the radio community and had stuck his neck out to get them to rehire Danny. I know Danny certainly respected John, and I knew it would weigh heavy on Danny if he let John down by getting into trouble.

Danny had a lot of appearances at night. I was diligent about accompanying him to these, as much as he didn't want me to sometimes. We had a real showdown about him hosting a bikini contest in a bar; he was emphatic that I not attend. I knew he would probably just be trying to hook up with the contestants and come home with lipstick smeared all over his face. I hadn't left him back in Phoenix, and this was his way of saying thanks. I was delighted when that appearance didn't renew their buy with the radio station.

After a few months living with his family, Danny and I had overstayed our welcome. We needed our own place.

We somehow scraped up enough money to buy a tiny little house in Manyunk, right on the Schuylkill River. It was over a century old and pretty beat up. Even so, I was thrilled to own my first house, let alone our first house together. I set out to paint every inch of it myself. I combed vintage and secondhand furniture stores and put together a cute little place for Danny and Max. Poor Maxi had been pretty much banished to the basement at Betty and Jackie's. Now he had a backyard all to himself to play in and was back sleeping between us.

On our first anniversary, Danny had made reservations at the cutest little restaurant that had been an old house built in the 1700s. The maitre d' walked us over to a corner table so we could enjoy our dinner quietly. When I looked down, the plates on the table were from one of my favorite artists Erte, the Russian/French art deco artist.

I looked up at Danny and said, "What a coincidence that you would take me to a place for our anniversary that uses this artist's work." Danny leaned over and whispered, "Steal them, put them in your purse when no one is looking." I was horrified. Like I would do such a thing. As it turned out, Danny knew that I liked his art and had found these plates at some flea market the day before. He drove to the restaurant early and dropped them off so they could serve our dinner on the plates. Every once in a while he would surprise me with sweet things like this.

In our own unique way, we were finally living the American dream, white picket fence and all.

Danny was usually off work early, so we would spend our days exploring the city. We both loved South Street and Little Italy. We were blessed to be living in a city rich with so much history that had occurred right in our own backyard: the homes of Ben Franklin and Betsy Ross, the Liberty Bell, Independence Hall, and Gettysburg nearby. Our first year of marriage was culminating, and it had rocked back and forth between bliss and bedlam, but maybe we were on the right track now.

I didn't make many friends while I was there—too busy babysitting my husband. I tried to work, but we had only one car. Besides, leaving him alone was still not a very good idea.

The best thing about living in Philly was being only an hour-and-a-half train ride from New York City. Danny was now on probation from the Phoenix incident, so every time we left the state, we once again had to ask permission. We found this out the hard way. Christmas Eve, Danny and I decided to take a drive. Since it was a holiday, there was no one to ask to get permission. Plus, honestly, we didn't think about it. We first drove up to the charming little town of Mystic, Connecticut, and had a romantic dinner. They sat us at a table by the warm fire. It was snowing, and the town glistened. We held hands and thanked our lucky stars for all the good things that had happened to us in the last few months. Danny was gainfully employed, we had a house, and we were in love (or at least as in love as Danny could be with someone).

After dinner we drove back to our motel on the water. That night, we watched the news in bed and saw a story where some dickhead had stolen this poor kid's wheelchair. Danny and I talked about it and decided we should buy him a new one. I called the news station and found out how to reach the family. The next morning, we drove to the guy's house and wrote him a check. I was thrilled that Danny and I were in the position to help someone in need. The TV station showed up and the local paper wrote an article about it.

A few days later when we returned to Philly, we had to report into the probation officer. I sat waiting while he went in. A few minutes passed. Then an hour. Then an hour and a half. At that point, some guy walked by me and said, "Hey, lady, they just arrested your husband."

I ran back to find someone of authority to ask, and sure enough, Danny had been arrested for violating his probation. We failed to get permission to leave the state, and they had a copy of the article about us being in Newport, Rhode Island. No good deed goes unpunished. Lucky for us, the probation officer decided under the circumstances he'd let it slide this once.

HOWARD STERN DOES NOT LIKE SURPRISES

A FEW WEEKS AFTER our Rhode Island scare, producers for Howard Stern thought it would be a great idea to surprise Howard with Danny showing up unexpectedly at a taping of his show. Of course, we remembered to ask permission to leave the state this time. I think they wanted Danny to challenge Howard to a fistfight or something like that.

Danny pushed through the door and got into a vicious verbal confrontation with Howard. Howard did not enjoy his "surprise" visit. I was so embarrassed for Danny—and myself—as Howard was less than thrilled to see us.

Years later, when Danny and I were doing *Breaking Bonaduce* on VH1, Howard said in print that it was his all-time favorite TV show. He was always so kind to me. I appreciated it because I knew he could be brutal if he wanted to be. I know it would have been so easy to make fun of me, but he never did.

I do recall Robin Quivers, Howard's sidekick, calling me a mental patient, though. Oh well, you win some, you lose some. Much prefer Howard on my side anyway.

We were up in New York quite often, as Danny continued doing the "ex-child-star-gone-wrong" shows for Sally Jesse Rafael, Richard Bay, and Maury Povich. We weren't getting Letterman and Conan offers at this point. In fact, acting as Danny's manager, I took every ridiculous TV offer I could get him to try to rebuild his reputation.

The weird thing that came out of that whole prostitute incident was a lot of TV exposure for Danny. Every time he was on a show making fun of himself, people loved him! There *is* no such thing as bad press, turns out.

Also, as a by-product of touring with David Cassidy, Danny had created a second side career doing stand-up several weekends a month, which was tough for me because clubs wouldn't pay for my ticket to fly with Danny. Financially, it didn't make sense to spend the profits on my flight as this extra income was slowly helping us dig out of debt. Danny didn't love doing stand-up, but the money was too good for him to turn down. I had been spoiled by my comedy background and was lucky enough to have seen the cream of the crop of up-and-coming comics. I didn't think his act was particularly funny, but nobody was funnier off the cuff than Danny. He always did a question-and-answer segment at the end of each set, and that was always the best part of the show.

Slowly, Danny was trying to be a man people could respect again. Things were going great. Unfortunately, I came to learn that this was a huge problem for Danny. This was when I needed to watch him the most. It was like a subconscious thing in his mind: "I'm doing great; time to shoot myself in the foot."

After about two years, the radio station began thinking of changing formats. Whenever this happens, stations typically blow out their entire lineup of DJs. If you were lucky, you had time left on your contract that they would have to pay off. But if they did that, they'd make sure you had a no-compete clause in your contract so you couldn't get another job on a radio station in the same city.

We asked Danny's radio agent, Lisa Miller, to start putting out the feelers. Danny had a *huge* following in Chicago thanks to Jonathon Brandmeier, Danny's friend and fellow DJ. Back in the early eighties, Johnny B had read an article about Danny being "dead broke and starving." Johnny had orchestrated a food drive in Chicago and had Danny flown in to host the event. When Danny arrived at the airport, fans were waiting at the gate with signs that read, "Stop hunger before it stops Danny Partridge!" Chicagoans seem to love Danny. We hoped WLUP in Chicago would have some interest in giving Danny a job— and they did.

Danny was offered the overnight slot on WLUP and once again we packed up Maxi and moved into a tiny little corporate apartment in downtown Chicago. I was going home! My friends and family all lived in the area. I could not have been more thrilled—or more frightened.

MEANWHILE, ON ANOTHER STATION, IN ANOTHER TOWN, IN SOME YEAR...

REMEMBER WHEN I SAID radio people can be the meanest bunch? At one point, Danny was paired with this bitch on wheels: Janis Black (not her real name). Now, let me tell you guys something. I have been around the block quite a few times and have met some of the best people on Earth, and some of the worst. When I tell you Janis Black was *absolutely* the most entitled, cruelest, meanest jerk I have ever met, I kid you not. I could not stand this woman, and I'm pretty sure from the day Danny started there she was trying to get him fired. She had the mouth of a sailor and always took the low road for the joke. It was excruciating to be in her presence, and I avoided her like the plague that she was. She and all of her friends were the worst lot I had ever met.

She was married but constantly boasted about having an affair, and that was the thing that killed me. She knew a lot of the stuff Danny was doing behind my back and did not respect that he would go on the radio day in and day out talking about his deep love for me. She would take it out on me for not knowing.

At least she was up-front about being a piece of shit. It made her blood boil that Danny was lying like that on the radio. And stupid, stupid me was buying the whole Danny lovefest like the rest of this town. It was weird for me because I had absolutely loved every other one of Danny's female partners. It was hard for me that his bigmouth jerk of a partner was someone I did not want to know any better.

Here is an example of one bit she did on the radio: "So, I was using my vibrator and some battery acid fell onto my meat curtains…" She actually said the words "meat curtains." Classy!

Or if she were talking about a subject that was way above her head, she would say something like: "During the trial the lawyer said, *some big word, some big word.*" She would actually say "some big word" because she didn't know how to pronounce it or the meaning. How did this idiot get on the radio?

While she was at the station, I know she bit a fan in the face at an appearance, and I understand they had to settle a pretty big lawsuit. A few years after Danny was let go from this particular radio station, she was arrested for a felony when she beat up her boyfriend with a golf club and put him in the hospital.

That said, the show was a pretty big success. They were doing well in the ratings. It was strange to me that Janis could never bite the bullet and understand that it was the chemistry between the two of them that made the show a hit. Miss Gigantic Ego thought it was all about her. It became kind of a popular segment on the show when Danny would call me. Well, that was the end of that! She couldn't stand the competition and rarely let him call me.

RENAISSANCE NIGHTS AND
THE KNIGHTS OF WRIGLEYVILLE

Sometime in 1988

ABOUT THIS TIME, JEFF, the gentleman recording me in Wisconsin, informed me that I'd need to move up his way if I wished to keep recording. I talk to Steph. She was such a pal and knew I wouldn't go alone, and so she offered to move with me.

I loved Chicago and wanted to move there. It was close enough to Wisconsin that I could still record with Jeff. My amazing roommate, Stephanie Morrison, the second most broken person I've ever met—Danny being hands down the first—offered to move there too. Steph was one of the most beautiful souls that I have ever had the privilege of knowing.

I met her in Phoenix, right after my ex-golf-pro boyfriend left me with a hefty rent to pay. She needed a place to stay, and with him gone, I had one. She moved in and we became best friends quickly, almost like female soul mates. We even adopted a stray kitty together that we named Desdemona. Steph turned me on to incredible bands like Nine Inch Nails, Ministry, and Echo & the Bunnymen.

We were super broke, so we just spent our time taking drives in my Jeep with the roof down, blaring music, hiking, going to free art galleries. She was an incredible artist and photographer.

She was dating a doctor at the time. He seemed to be captivated by her free spirit; she was certainly hard to pin down. I think he had treated her at one of those urgent care places and that was where they'd met, as Steph and I did not run in the doctor/lawyer Scottsdale crowd. A very unlikely duo, indeed. He wanted her bad, and she basically blew him off, which only served to make him want her more.

Somehow, one day, we were able to scrape enough money together to go to the Renaissance Fair outside of Phoenix. We made fast friends with some of the knights. You have not lived until you wake up to gorgeous men in chainmail jousting in the living room. Many evenings I awoke to the sounds of swords clinking and fake European accents. *Huzzah! Fetch me my mead, you wench!*

Fall 1987

BUT FIRST, WE TAKE a trip to LA. I had never been and was so excited to experience Tinseltown. We flew into LAX, where we were going to be picked up by her friends from Orange County, who were also giving us a place to stay. Somehow, we missed them. After waiting a few hours, we decided we needed to formulate a Plan B. Around this time, quite possibly the most devastatingly handsome man I have ever seen in person (I mean, I've seen guys this good-looking on TV, but never in person) walks by me and smiles. I look around to see who the lucky woman must be earning a smile from movie-star good-looking guy.

I look. There's no one standing there but me. I manage a weak and uncomfortable smile and then turn around and run over to Steph.

"Steph," I say, "you've got to see the best-looking guy I have ever seen." I motion over to where he is standing. "Look!"

She makes a beeline to him.

I'm saying, "Steph, Steph, no!" under my breath. Who knows what my kookie friend will pop off?

She waltzes up to him, and in a fake British accent (she loves talking in an affected British accent for no reason—Madonna, meet Steph. Steph, meet Madonna) says, "Excuse me, sir, my friend and I have no ride, and we were wondering if you thought it would be a bad idea for us to hitchhike to the OC (LA slang for Orange County)." And the gorgeous tan man with the flowing reddish-brown mane and the cutest button nose goes, "Ya, I think that would be a really, really bad idea. Tell ya what. My car just got towed. I have to walk to the police station and get it out. If you want to come with me, I'll take you to my house in Hollywood, and you can make arrangements to meet up with your friends there." Not only did he look like an angel from a medieval painting, but he turned out to be our real-life angel!

I can't fathom that a guy who wants to rape and murder us would take us to the police station first. I'm all for this plan. On the way, he introduces himself—Ashton (not his real name). Eventually, we get his 1959 Mercedes out and head to his place. He has a cute little apartment off of La Brea and Franklin in Hollywood. We can't reach her friends, and so he makes us dinner while singing opera to us. Seriously, I am not making this up.

Over dinner he tells us that actually he is a CIA agent and also a video director. Whenever I have told this story, without exception people ask me what kind of an idiot I am that I would fall for such a tall tale.

Guys, you didn't see this guy! You would have fallen for it, too!

After dinner, Steph reaches her friends, and they are not willing to drive back in traffic to get us. Dammit, but not really. I'm thrilled because Ashton offers to put us up for the night. I cannot believe our luck. I am absolutely mesmerized by this CIA agent/video director.

The only problem is, we have to share his bed. You guys have to remember, I have never been considered a particularly pretty/beautiful/gorgeous person. The best I could ever get was "she's a cute girl." This has boosted my ego and I'm not letting go.

Now my problem was going to be how to get rid of Steph and get Ashton all to myself.

He seemed to kinda be hitting on both of us. I whispered under my breath, "I saw him first, Steph. Hands off!" I could listen to this guy all night. But it's getting late.

We all pile into bed and go to sleep (I'm sure this is not where you thought this was going). And yes, we *sleep*. That is all.

Over the next two days we don't leave his place and end up forging a friendship that would last a few years. This man's friendship—and that's all it ever was, he wasn't romantically interested in me—meant a great deal to me. He was the first guy who took me places and acted as though I were the most beautiful girl in the room. (I never was.) He was the first—and only, I might add—guy to actually lift up my Jeep using only his hands to change a tire. He made me feel smart, interesting. The confidence building I did on this man's arm was rather astounding.

Ashton had the patience of Job when I was practically stalking and harassing him. He was never cross or unkind to me when he had every right to be. A year later, I was watching MTV and saw him starring in a video. He was THAT good-looking.

I never got to thank him for that. Ashton, I thought you were the bee's knees and always will. You will always be my CIA agent/video director. I believe you.

After I married Danny, I couldn't be friends with him. Danny never met him but hated his guts just for meaning so much to me. Steph stayed in touch with him for years. I know he always asked about me. I don't know what ever happened to him. But if you're reading this, Ashton, I hope you know you meant a great deal to me and always will. And just in case you were actually telling the truth all along, I have changed your name—I don't want to blow your cover.

Steph and I get back to Phoenix and pack up all of our things in our cars, making a pit stop at Mom and Dad's to say goodbye.

Spring 1988

AND SO WE TREK across the United States in our little car caravan.

We arrived at Granny's a few days later and settled in. I started work almost immediately and Steph had lined up a job in Evanston at an art gallery.

Remember our Renaissance knights? Who knew months later these knights would come to our rescue in Chicago with a place to sublet on Addison Avenue, right next to Wrigley Field. They were leaving shortly to do their nationwide tour and agreed to let us move in once they left for the summer. They had a third-story walk-up right next door to the sports corner bar on Addison and Sheffield, and if we sat on the roof of the old brownstone we could almost see over the top to watch the game.

If we turned on the TV, we could see the top rows of the stands AND hear the game.

We loved Chicago!

Unfortunately, my deal with Jeff, the music guy in Kenosha, ended up going away, but no matter. We were doing a lot more in Chicago than we'd ever done in Phoenix. The possibilities seemed endless in the windy city.

Except, within a month, Steph lost her job at the art gallery and was on the hunt for a new one. This would be the first of many lost jobs for my poor roomie. Then, three or four weeks into our sublease, Steph's sister Susan informed us she needed to leave her summer job in Martha's Vineyard and move in with us, too.

We, of course, allowed her to move in with us, followed two weeks later by her new boyfriend. So now it was me, Steph, her sister Susan, and her new boyfriend Ron. This did not sit well with the knights. They had agreed two girls could move in, not three and some guy. They insisted we move out.

This was okay with me, as we were right next to the L tracks, where bums love to set up camp. Just a few nights before I had been walking in late from work and a drunk bum tried to slash me in the face with a broken bottle. I had never been so frightened—until a few nights later when a guy followed me off the L and tried to attack me. I was shaking so bad and was just grateful I was able to get in the security door and slam it shut. He slammed against it and tried to open it. I shudder to think what would have happened to me had he been successful.

I was not at all upset about moving off that street. Until we ended up moving to a more dangerous place in Irving Park, which served as the only neutral block between the Latin Kings and another rival gang. So Steph, Suz, Ron, and now another one of their friends from Martha's Vineyard, Ted, and I all moved into a two-bedroom, second-story apartment that shared a wall with the L track. We literally could have put a hand out the window and touched the L as it drove by. It shook the whole apartment every time the train would pass, which was quite a bit.

We slept pretty much anywhere we could find space—a bunch of wadded-up clothes and blankets on the floor. During the winter we would leave the stove on with the door open to warm it up.

Bad, bad idea. I can't believe we didn't burn the place down.

We had made friends with one of the cops who patrolled our street when Steph and I went around a barricade and ended up at the end of the Gay Pride parade. We didn't know the parade was happening that day and we needed to get to the other side of town, so naturally we jumped out and moved the barricade and took our spot at the end of the parade. We got across town and had fun in the parade, even though neither of us were gay.

Steph and I would bake the Chicago PD chocolate chip cookies in hopes that they would look after us and not tow our cars. Unfortunately, that corner of Irving Park was a very popular place for TV and film productions to film, so our cars were towed all the time.

I took a second job working at a bar that I'm pretty sure the mob frequented. The owner loved to put all the most popular booze on the actual top shelf so that I had to climb up the ladder to get them down. Of course, he would seat his friends directly across from there and order Frangelico so that they could try to look up my skirt.

Pig.

But the tips were decent, and I needed all the financial help I could get at that point. I was able to get Steph a job there as a favor to me after she had been fired from yet another job. I will go on record saying Steph was the worst bartender I had ever seen. Her drinks were just the worst, most poorly put together combinations of alcohol I had ever witnessed. I worked that job and Alamo as long as I could, sometimes not getting home until two or three in the morning and having to be at Alamo at six.

One morning I woke up and went out to get my car. As usual it had been towed. Jeez, these productions were starting to piss me off! I called the number to find my car.

The gentleman on the line said, "Ma'am, your car has been repossessed." Funny guy. "Ha-ha," I said. "Where's my car?"

"Uh, lady, not kidding. Your car was repossessed for nonpayment." And he hung up on me.

That effectively ended my job at Alamo, as I could not get out to O'Hare from downtown without a car. That left me with waiting tables at the mob bar.

What to do. What to do.

Suz worked at the Improv Comedy Club downtown and heard the comedy club around the corner called the Funny Firm was hiring. I applied for the job, and thank the Lord I got it! At least I could take the L downtown and get there with no problem. I was elated to be working at such a fun place with three different comics every week.

The first night I worked was crazy. It was a two-drink minimum per customer. They slammed your section with fifty or sixty people all at once. Trying to get all the drinks right and be sure everyone had at least two of them was hard work. The first night as I was cashing out, I realized I had a walk out. It had never occurred to me that someone would do that. No one had warned me to watch my section because at the end of the night it was total chaos when dropping bills, and people might slip out if they could get away with it. All the tips I made that night I had to give to the bar. I was devastated. I really needed that money. But once again, that's just me. Never wanted to believe anything bad about anyone, and it never occurred to me that someone might try to dodge a bill.

I almost quit that night, but one of the sweet waitresses talked me out of it. I decided to go back one more night and try again. I'm so glad I did. Aside from being a candy striper, it was the best job I ever had. I made friends with a lot of the comics and the other wait staff there. The waiters and waitresses were kind of the comics' family when on the road.

Several months in, I started to feel stagnant in Chicago. Steph had become too much for me to handle. I couldn't take care of myself, let alone take care of my friend. She was struggling to get along. The whole time I knew her she was always sick. She had been diagnosed with infantigo, a staph infection, everything under the sun. She had these lesions on her face that she could not get to go away no matter what kinds of cream or meds she was on.

Many years later, after I married Danny, we reconnected. She'd had such a hard life. She told me she was living in a homeless shelter in Denver. She called me and said she was moving to Latin America so that she could afford her medication. She had hooked up with this alternative clinic that diagnosed her as one of the first people in the nation with a flesh-eating bacterial infection.

They were treating her with radio waves. I didn't like the sound of it.

On her way to somewhere in Latin America, she stopped to meet my new son, Count Dante. (My second baby. Isabella was my first. You'll meet them in a minute.)

When I saw her, I almost started to weep. This once vibrant, beautiful woman looked like a very ill homeless person. Her nose was beak-like. I could see all the muscles in her face. Her eyelashes and eyebrows were all gone. She asked me if she could store some of her things at my house. I had to say no because we were storing Danny's brother's things and there was no room in our garage for anything else. As she drove off, I didn't realize it would be the last time I would ever see her.

She would pop back in and out of LA a few times, but it never worked out that we could get together. She had befriended the guy who played Boner on *Family Ties* (only Steph would find the most random people) and usually stayed with him while she was in LA.

I received a voice mail one day from her sister. She was crying and told me to call her. I already knew. I knew this would not be a good call. I started shaking as I dialed her number, she picked up the phone and informed me that Steph had been killed. I was shocked. Yet not entirely surprised. When we lived together, we put ourselves into bad situations all the time. Like if we locked ourselves out of our place, we would climb up to the second story L tracks, walk across the tracks without touching them, and swing from the second story into our open window. Or walk through deserted graveyards in the middle of the night to take a short cut from the Metro/Smart bar in Chicago to our apartment. We thought we were invincible and behaved as if no one or thing could harm us. She in particular always saw the good in people, no matter their station. There wasn't an ulterior-motive bone in her body. She was too amazing to be confined to a human body, she really needed to be free of all human constraints. And now she was.

It was time for me to leave Chicago. Back to Mom and Dad's in Phoenix for the second time—where I'd meet and marry Danny.

CHI-TOWN, PART DEUX

Spring 1993

EXCITED, YES. SCARED, YES. Why, you ask?

Well, as I previously mentioned. I married a very jealous man. I even had a conversation with him that went like this:

"Uh, are you going to be a dick if we run into anyone I've dated?" I asked Danny.

"Uh, ya. If we even run into someone that knows a guy you went out with, I'm going to go sideways," he answered.

Oh boy.

Thank God I dated very few guys while I lived in Chicago. That turned out to be a very big upside to having such a crush on my CIA agent/video director. I wasn't interested in too many guys because of my delusional crush on Ashton.

Danny started working what they call overnights, so I adjusted my schedule to fit his. Up all night. Asleep most of the day. We ended up moving into this cool loft apartment on Printer's Row, and I was able to reconnect with all of my Chicago friends.

One night we went to the Improv to visit my old roommate Suz, aka Susan, Steph's sister. I didn't like the way Danny was acting that night. I couldn't put my finger on it, but something seemed off.

A few days later, Suz and another girlfriend who'd been at our wedding and who I had worked with at the Funny Firm, called me. Apparently that night, while at the Improv, Danny had walked up to one of the waitresses and said, "I'm Danny, and I'm married but I cheat on my wife all the time."

I don't know if she told them because she knew they were my friends and she thought I should know this, or if she was bragging about it. Either way, it got back to me. Of course, Danny went into protection mode and claimed the girl was lying and wanted me to break off my friendships for telling me. Gaslighting. Yep. Classic case.

Girls, this is what an abuser does. He tries to isolate you from everyone. Especially people who are not afraid to tell you the truth. They *will* be your friends and tell you things the abuser doesn't want you to know. And the abuser will demand you make a choice. Well, if I wanted to stay in my marriage, there was no choice but to cut them out of my life. My friends had nothing to lose by telling me, except being friends with me. I regret that I let Danny bulldoze me into that.

More apologies owed to Susan and Lisa. (I guess this is going to be a book with a lot of apologies.)

This should never, ever be the case. No one should have to apologize to people because of her partner's behavior. Many, many times Danny would act like a jerk and I would be left to apologize to others. It would embarrass me so much when he would act like a rude asshole, and I spent quite a bit of our marriage apologizing on his behalf.

On the bright side, Danny's overnight show was turning into a big hit! After a few months they moved him to late nights—starting at seven o'clock and winding down around midnight. Of all the radio shows Danny had done, WLUP was my favorite. It was such a fun, interesting show.

But once again, I had to apply pressure to keep him out of trouble. He came home one night chewing his cheek again. I demanded the keys and went to look for evidence in his car.

He was sweating bullets and wouldn't let me have the keys until he went outside. So he left for work and took a cab, as I needed to go grocery shopping so he had to leave me the car. As he was driving away in the cab, I checked around our car. Underneath the car next to ours was an aluminum foil package. I'm not stupid. I knew he cleaned out the car and threw it there so I wouldn't find it in the car. I was livid! When things were going great—that was his pattern to mess it up.

I'm sure many people thought I got what I deserved. Marry a guy you don't know? You had it coming. But as I saw it, I married someone I felt in love with and who happened to be a screwed-up man with a lifetime of bad habits and an unbelievable sense of entitlement. And, somehow, I thought I could help him unlearn this bad behavior, even if it took years. If I could change him at all.

These warning signs were actually good—they alerted me that he was sliding so I could jump on him quickly. I had hoped he would see the benefits of trying to live a truthful life, that it would eventually stick for good. After all, people were starting to respect him. Finally! And that's why I worked hard at helping to keep him straight.

1993

DANNY'S CONTRACT KEPT GETTING extended, so we thought it was time for us to buy our second house. We found a charming house off of Irving Park Road. It looked like a tiny French château.

We had at this point paid off the legal debt in Phoenix and Danny was doing so well in ratings his time slot kept getting moved up. We could afford it.

Not long after, we found out the stork was going to be visiting us. It was a Saturday afternoon and we were going to see Davy Jones from The Monkees in the touring show of *Grease*.

I was very *very* skinny when we moved to Chicago. Ninety-eight pounds, in fact. I was trying very hard to quit smoking at the time and had never been on birth control the whole time I was married to Danny. But I guess everything does happen when it's supposed to. I doubt the past four years would have been a great thing for me to be pregnant and try to take care of a kid while I was fighting so hard to get Danny under control.

I hoped so much that God would bless us with a child. It was my little girl dream to grow up and get married and have children.

Maybe I felt this so strongly because both my grandmother and mother died in or following childbirth. That would either make you never want to have children—or long to have them and love them with all your heart. The latter was my way.

When I thought of starting my own family, it was hard not to recall the terror of that day my mother died a few days after giving birth to my sister. She was married to Rex then, and I was only seven years old. One morning, I awoke to the sound of army boots and dark shadows running underneath my closed bedroom door. I tried to listen but could not hear what they were saying. After a few minutes, I heard their boots heading for the door. I opened my door as they were leaving. The sound of army boots on a wooden floor will forever stay seared in my memory.

I tiptoed out and saw my stepfather sitting on the sofa crying. I had never seen a grown man cry before.

"What's wrong?" I asked.

He moved the pillow over on the couch and said, "Sit down, Gretchen." Then he added, "Your mother has died."

About this time, my brother came out of his room and saw me hysterically crying. I blurted out the terrible news. We just sat there crying, not fully comprehending the situation.

Rex did not make us go to school that day. I remember playing in the playground and after school all the kids walking by, asking us if it was true that our mother had died. Bad news travels fast.

We were told that childbirth had just been too hard on her body and she had passed away. My baby sister Aimee had survived, but she would never know her mother.

A few days later we were on a plane back to the United States with friends of my parents as Rex was in no shape to take care of an infant and two stepchildren. We arrived back at O'Hare Airport to bring my mother's body home.

It never even occurred to me that my mother was in the cargo hold under the plane.

That trip made me recall the excitement of the day we flew to Germany after she married Rex. My mother was afraid to fly, and I kept assuring her it would be fine. With my flights to Phoenix, I was an old pro. Maybe she was so scared because she somehow knew she wouldn't be coming back, at least not alive.

Between O'Hare and my mother's funeral, I couldn't tell you a thing. I must have wiped out that entire timeframe of my life.

The day of the funeral I remember walking in and seeing her closed casket. Because I had not seen her body, I would have nightmares for years that she wasn't really dead and just didn't want us anymore.

Years later, when I was twenty-two, I learned what really happened that day my mother died—or what I think happened, based on letters and things I've heard over the years. Truthfully, I'm not exactly sure what happened to her. (If you happen to know and are reading this book, please contact me.)

I have a letter from a lady, Judy—she and her husband were the couple that flew back from Germany with us. She said in the letter that when my mother was having my sister, she died on the table. Miraculously, they were able to somehow bring her back. I think maybe she had been dead for too long and when they did bring her back, maybe her brain had been oxygen deprived for too long. Judy said that for about a week she didn't recognize anyone or know where she was.

Judy said she seemed to be coming out of it a bit and asked her to bring back some food from home. I guess she was not a fan of German hospital cuisine. Judy left to go home and make her some soup. Somehow, after Judy left, my mother fell out of the window and died. I don't know if she jumped, or if she still wasn't okay and accidently fell. I guess I may never know.

She died at twenty-six. I have had double that in years on this planet. She was robbed of so many things—proms, weddings, the births of her grandkids. I know my mother loved me, but I don't remember her saying it. It was one thing I wanted so much.

To be sure that my kids would always have a memory of me *telling* them I love them, we created the "I love you spot" nearby our house. Every time we pass a particular spot on the street, we all yell "I LOVE

YOU!" In case something ever happened to me, I needed my kids to have that memory because I don't have that.

∗∗∗

I WAS PUTTING ON weight and wasn't feeling well. During one of Danny's commercial breaks, I called him and told him I was going to take a pregnancy test. He begged me to take it on the air. I thought, the people of Chicago have been so wonderful to us; it would be great to share this moment with them. I agreed to do it, and drove to the store to buy a pregnancy test.

We lived by Koreatown. The smell of kimchi was thick in the air and I was trying to make it home before I started to blow chunks. To this day I can't smell kimchi without feeling nauseated. It was the unfortunate by-product of my morning sickness. Negative association. I called Danny and went into the bathroom with him live on the air.

I peed. And we waited.

A few minutes went by and I started to see the faintest line! We were going to be parents!

That evening I met him at *Grease*, and he picked me up and scooped me into his arms. He got down on his knees and introduced himself to my belly. *Hi, baby! I'm your daddy!*

I am sure all couples feel this intense love for one another when they find they are having a baby together, and we were no exception. I threw myself into learning every single thing I could about pregnancy. I doubt there was a book written I didn't read. I immediately stopped smoking and drinking. It wasn't too hard; I had such awful morning sickness that everything made me want to throw up. I slept with my hands around my tummy just hugging my baby. Danny threw himself in too, and we called our baby Swimmer. *Swimmer was doing flips today, Swimmer was kicking me hard, Swimmer wants Mommy to eat chocolate.*

I have to say, it was the happiest I ever was with Danny.

Danny went to Lamaze classes with me. It turned out two of my comic friends from the Funny Firm were in our class. You definitely want two stand-up comics in your Lamaze class, if you have a choice. Every time we had to watch one of those birthing films, those two were so full of hilarious comments. Some girl would be pushing out some kid on the film and her partner would be a hero with encouragement. My comic friends wondered what that guy was doing on her birthday. They wanted him at their birth! When you're already having bladder control problems from being pregnant, all you need is two smart-ass comics making jokes.

It is a scientific fact that your brain shrinks while you are pregnant, and I was emotional all the time. Danny and his father had been estranged for years and years and I wanted him to try and repair their relationship now that we were going to be having a child. I thought our baby should have a relationship with her grandfather. Danny's father, Joe, happened to be taking a trip to Italy in 1994 and was going to schedule a layover in Chicago and stay with us for a few days. We picked him up and had a nice dinner with him at a restaurant. Danny and Joe seemed to be reconnecting. During the middle of dinner, Joe broke down crying and apologized to Danny for never liking him.

The next evening, Danny had a meeting with our friend Kevin Trudeau (you guys remember, the Mega Memory guy from the infomercials), so I stayed at home and made dinner with Joe and tried to get to know him a little better. As the hours went by, I started to grow a little concerned that Danny had not returned home. These were the days before everyone had a cell phone. Since I had become pregnant, he was pretty diligent about getting home early to be with me. As the evening wore on, I didn't realize that my alarm was starting to upset Joe. I had always heard the stories about Joe's temper but had never witnessed it. I did not realize that my hysteria was making Joe very upset.

I started calling the hospitals, and the police, as I was worried something was wrong. I could not fathom that Danny would behave like this with his father in town. Finally, around four in the morning, Danny rolled up in Kevin Trudeau's brand-new Ferrari. I came flying out the door with my shoe in my hand and started beating the hood of the car with my shoe. Kevin began yelling at Danny to get out of his car and finally Danny got out and headed inside where he was met by his father screaming at him, "Gretchen is sacred and carrying my grandchild" and that Danny was incredibly disrespectful to leave me at home this late. Then he bunched up his fist and punched Danny square in the face.

I have always felt incredibly guilty about that. Joe was defending me and it caused things to get worse between them. I thought it an odd choice for him to do that while his father was visiting. It's the one thing I guess I could always count on: that Danny would usually make the wrong choice. Joe left the next morning, and they rarely spoke after that.

***

I WAS SO EXCITED when it was time to get my ultrasound. Danny didn't want to know, so I wasn't going to tell him, but I couldn't wait to find out. The nurse ran the thing over my tummy and announced it would be a girl.

I squealed in uncontrollable delight! The doctor who would be delivering my baby was about eighty years old and had been a missionary doctor in Africa. He had delivered babies under the worst of circumstances and I felt completely safe in his hands. I didn't seem to have any fears related to childbirth, even given my family history— my mother and grandmother both having died soon after childbirth. Medicine had advanced so much since then. However, we did not agree on the way my child should come into this world: I wanted a cesarean section. When we discussed it, he informed me I had an adequate uterus and I would be just fine.

This infuriated me. How dare you, Mr. Average Penis. I know you meant to say that it was the finest uterus you had ever seen. Adequate my ass! I was so insulted. In any event, he refused to give me my way.

I had talked Danny into buying another house as an investment in the suburbs of Chicago. We had found this gorgeous house that had been a construction demo. The builder wanted to showcase every top-notch thing you could have built in your home. It had two full kitchens, an indoor pool, wet and dry sauna, and a beautiful hand-carved library.

I especially loved the pool. When my parents were getting their divorce, they sent my brother Kurt and me to stay with my dad's parents in Phoenix. My grandparents lived in an apartment with a nice pool. The smell of hot wet pavement always brings me back to that little apartment. Weird how certain smells will take you back in time. I still love that smell—it reminds me of my childhood.

Our house sat on five acres and had a pond stocked with fish and a chapel on the grounds. During the winter we would sit in the hot tub and watch the snow fall. At night in the summer the fireflies lit up the evening sky. Two weeks before Isabella was scheduled to arrive, we moved into our new home. I was hoping it would expedite her arrival and tried to move as much as I could myself.

As my stomach grew, I could no longer sleep flat because of the terrible acid reflux. I hated being pregnant and could not wait for my little girl to come out and play with her mommy. On her due date, I went in to see the doc. He thought I should give it another week. She hadn't dropped yet.

I was having none of it! This was my due date and she was coming out, come hell or high water. At 10:00 a.m., they hooked me up to Pitocin. By 2:00 p.m., my water had not broken so they had to do it. I don't think they had given me the epidural at that point because I remember that as being very painful. When they came in to give me the epidural, I was very grateful. All these granola folks who want to enjoy their birth process—not for me. I didn't enjoy it until the epidural.

I started pushing around 3:00 p.m. Perfect timing, as Danny was just getting off the air from WLUP. He was going to make it in time. My daughter was so stubborn she did not want to come out. Foreshadowing, I suppose. They tried forceps, and even attempted to vacuum her out. She was not ready for her close-up yet.

Finally, around 7:00 p.m., she gave up and decided to make an appearance. She had her pouty lip so far out…and made one small cry, and that was it. I was in love.

Countess Isabella Michaela Bonaduce had entered the world. Six pounds, seven ounces. She looked up at me with her gooey eyes and didn't know what to make of me. I told her how wanted and loved she was. I had never, ever been so happy in my life. I made them move the incubator into my room because I couldn't stand for her to be away from me.

The next morning was Thanksgiving and I just wanted to go home. Danny came to bring his little family back to the huge mansion in Barrington Hills that I had talked him into buying. I'll never forget the first day he came back home from work after we brought her home. I couldn't find him; I searched the house and found him in Isabella's room sitting in the rocking chair with her. It melted my heart. I could see in his face that he had never loved anything or anyone more.

A perfect day to start our new beginning.

Thanksgiving. I was very grateful.

We had managed to clean up Danny's public image so well that Buena Vista TV was offering him his own TV show. From almost prison to Disney! That was an incredible jump and spoke volumes of Danny's talent as a performer. The show would shoot in Chicago and be called *Danny!*

Things were about to get busy.

The bosses at WLUP had given him the afternoon-drive time slot so that it was possible for him to shoot the TV show in the morning and early afternoon and still do radio. He was shooting TV three days a week and doing radio five days. It was actually good for him—so much work helped me to help him to stay out of trouble. He was exhausted by the weekend. I could not have been prouder.

The show came out at a time when everyone had a show. Mark Walberg, Gabrielle Carteris, Carnie Wilson. It was a very crowded space to try to get ratings in. It was your standard TV fare. "I'm fat and all that" and "Who's the baby daddy?" You know, super highbrow stuff. That year, with the competition for ratings fierce, they were scraping the bottom of the barrel for show ideas. It was the reign of *The Jerry Springer Show* and shows had to follow suit to compete.

Unfortunately for us, the show lasted only six months. He just couldn't get enough ratings for Disney to keep shooting. We were disappointed, but life goes on. Within six months of the show failing, the company that owned WLUP decided to slide Danny into the morning slot in Detroit.

So, once again, Danny was doing two jobs! And we were on the move again. The mansion in Barrington Hills made the commute too difficult. We had to get an apartment downtown and commute. We found a great place in Lake Point Towers.

So, during the week, we lived there to make things easier for Danny and went home on the weekends. Pretty cushy life, right?

I DIE FOR DI!

BACK IN 1996, LADY Di came to Chicago for a fundraiser. I was beside myself with excitement, as I was quite possibly the world's biggest Lady Di fan. Come hell or high water, I was determined to meet the princess. Lucky for me, one of Danny's radio colleagues, Harry Tinowitz, was a good friend of the catering manager at the Drake Hotel, where she would be staying. Harry made a call on my behalf and we set a plan in motion.

The morning of the fundraiser, I agonized over my wardrobe. What in the world does one wear to meet a princess?

No. Not a princess. *The* princess. The princess of all princesses.

I finally settled on a conservative suit that was handmade by Mira Couture for Danny's TV show in Chicago, *Danny!,* and headed for the Drake. I knew security was going to be tight and I wanted to be sure I left myself plenty of time. When I arrived, the catering manager came down to meet me, and he knew exactly what door Diana was going to come out to go to the banquet.

We located a child in the crowd who had a bouquet. The manager placed the girl in front of the door as we were sure she would head over to the little girl to take the flowers. He strategically placed me right behind her. At the designated hour, the door opened and out she came. It was like something out of a movie. She hit her mark and walked right over to the little girl in front of me.

I thought I was going to faint! She was even more lovely in person.

Now, anyone who knows anything about royal protocol knows you are not supposed to speak to royalty unless spoken to first. So naturally I lost all sense of decorum and began yelling, "Welcome to Chicago!

We love you, Lady Di!" I'm not sure what else I may have blurted, as I sort of blacked out for a few seconds there, having realized my royal faux pas.

She bent down and took the flowers from the little girl, glancing at me with a rather odd look. She quickly made her way down the hallway, stopping here and there to say hello to the crowd of people not lucky enough to possess tickets to her event. Afterward, the catering manager told me a story about how she had ordered room service and the waiter who delivered her order was named Jesus.

I guess she laughed and laughed that Jesus had delivered her tea to her. Oohhhh, I just loved her.

After she returned back to London, they auctioned the room off at another charity auction. Danny outbid everyone to be sure I would get the room! We threw a small dinner party the night we stayed there, and of course had to take pictures of us on the toilet as Di's tushy had been seated on it at one point.

When she passed away a year later, I cried and cried for a week.

I for one am very excited that America will have a new princess in a few months. I am absolutely in love with Meghan Markle and Prince Harry. I wonder if Princess Di would approve?

Chicago was one of the happiest times I think we had as a family. Now I had my own little Disney Princess.

It was fun to take Isabella to Navy Pier every day. When she was little she just loved the movie *Pocahontas*. She would watch it over and over. She couldn't say the word Pocahontas, but instead called it Koko me.

I took her out for a walk one day. There was a kiosk that sold books and they had a *Pocahontas* book.

"Moooommy! Koko me!" she cried.

"Yes, Isabella, Koko me. Would you like the book?"

"Yes. Me want Koko me!"

Of course I bought it for her. A couple of days later, I took her back and she saw the book again. She had the most colossal meltdown. No matter how much I tried to explain there was more than one book she was convinced there was only one book and they had her copy. "Mine, mommy. My Koko meeeeee!"

A few months into the WLUP and Detroit job, the radio station decided we needed to move permanently to Detroit. Ugh. Such is the life of radio. So we packed up and moved to Motown.

*Me practicing ballet in the 1970s.
I was already showing signs of SOS: show off syndrome.*

*Isabella and me backstage at her daddy's TV show
DANNY! in Chicago.*

Dante joining me onstage at Citywallk.

Danny and me on the set of America's Deadliest Home Video, *where I played his wife.*

*Our wedding in Phoenix, AZ, May 4, 1991, at the Cresent Hotel.
Left to right: John and Anthony Bonaduce, Danny's high school best friends, Scott and Dave,
Celia Bonaduce, Danny and me, my best friend, Rachel, my sister, Aimee, and Julie.*

*A photo from our first wedding on November 4 in Pheonix.
Wedding dounts and cheap champagne from 7-Eleven to toast the occasion.*

Danny on the air with John Margolis, The Eagle 106, in Philadelphia.

Danny and me in what can only be described as the honeymoon phase.
Ignorance is indeed bliss.

Me and Stuttering John Melendez after the surprise attack on Howard's E! show.

Danny and me on the set of The Other Half *with Dick Clark.*

Lemmy and me at the Rainbow Bar and Grill on Sunset Boulevard.

Me, Alanis Morissette, and Danny at the Star 98.7 Not So Silent Night, December 17, 2001.

The unbelievable Cherie Currie and me with my band Ankh at the Hard Rock Cafe Hollywood. What superstar legend will get up and sing with you at a show? Cherie. End of list.

The Muddflaps. Great musicians and wonderful people. Bob, Chris Doohan, and Page.

Kevin, me, Rodney Bingenheimer, and his friend, playing the Highway to Help benefit at The Viper Room with Gay C/DC and Street Walking Cheetahs.

P IS FOR PIE
(NOT THE P YOU WERE
EXPECTING I'M SURE)

NOW THAT DANNY WAS a father, he wanted to get in shape and start living a better life. I supported anything positive that Danny came up with. Trading off the drug addiction, Danny decided to work a fitness addiction instead. He'd work out for hours and hours and try to eat sensibly. Well, the eating sensibly was going to be difficult for me. I'm the kind of girl who eats candy for breakfast and a big piece of pie for lunch.

I did my best to buy only healthy things and cook nutritious meals for Danny. But sometimes I could not resist the urge to buy something special for myself. In Chicago, during the fall, you could go to the apple orchards and pick your own apples. Some of these places had the most beautiful and delicious apple pies you've ever seen. I wanted one. I knew this was forbidden contraband, but my desire for a piece of that pie outweighed my promise to not buy junk. My plan was to make the pie a traveling pie and move its location from hiding place to hiding place.

One day I heard my name bellowed from the basement.

"GRETCHEN! GRETCHEN!!!!"

Oh shit.

I knew that tone could only mean one thing.

I ran down the stairs, clutching our baby, Isabella, in my arms. When I reached the bottom of the stairs, Danny just stood there with the pie in his hands. I ran toward him, and in the smoothest move I could manage, I slid Isabella in his arms and removed the pie from his hands.

He and Isabella started to chase me. We ran around the pool table and all over the basement while he yelled at me to return the pie to him. He wanted some, and I had better give it to him. I had to think fast. What could I throw on the pie that would make him not eat it! I looked for the ashtray to dump cigarette butts on the pie. No luck. No ashtray on hand.

I ran toward the garbage can. I was going to dump the garbage can on the beautiful pie. He blocked me.

Uh-oh. He'd pushed me to the limit.

I had no choice.

I threw the pie on the ground and sat on it. I started to pee on the pie.

Everything went silent for a moment. Then we erupted into uncontrollable laughter. I had successfully stopped him from eating the pie. The next day he told the story on the air and it became legend. It also became code to our friends for "being broke"—i.e., "I'm so broke I don't even have pie to pee on."

ST. LUCIA: DID YOU READ THE HERMAN WOAK BOOK, DON'T STOP THE CARNIVAL? THIS PUTS IT TO SHAME

Spring 1995

ONE OF THE MANY harebrained ideas that Danny and I had at one point was to buy property in a foreign country for vacation purposes, figuring we could rent it out when we were not there. We set out looking at a few Caribbean islands to invest in. Our first thought was Anguilla. We found a beautiful beachfront piece of land that we could build our house on. We had no idea what it would entail, and so I set out to educate myself about buying property in a foreign land. We had to put the property in my name, as some of the islands would not let you buy if you had a criminal record—and guess who had one of those?

It was a relatively easy process. We gave them a deposit and filled out the necessary paperwork for the government to approve us. You couldn't just buy there—they had to say you were acceptable to do so. We put a check down to hold the beautiful little piece of real estate where we would build our dream vacation home.

When we returned to Chicago, after much thought, we decided to pull the deal as we were not sure the timing was right. I wish we had gone through with that sale. Anguilla is still one of my very favorite islands in the Caribbean.

And mostly importantly, it would have perhaps saved us from St. Lucia.

It would have been a better idea to book a cabin on the *Titanic* than to buy this piece of property!

St. Lucia is one of the Windward Islands of the Lesser Antilles, between Martinique and St. Vincent, and north of Barbados. Danny and I had never been able to afford a honeymoon after our wedding, and so when one of his radio sponsors gave us a deal to go to Sandals St. Lucia, we jumped at the chance. As we flew over, we looked out the window and saw the volcanic spires—"The Pitons"—and the lush greenery of St. Lucia.

We took a shuttle to Sandals and settled into our room. What a lovely place! One of the things I love about Sandals is that it is all-inclusive. Everything you want to do is included in the price. Most vacations, by the second day I am trying to figure out what not to do because I start thinking about the cost. With Sandals, you don't even think about it, because you're not spending any money at all. Not even tipping is permitted.

One of the excursions that we went on was a snorkeling trip. They took us to a tiny place called Shingle Cove where we found three of the most charming little houses. It turned out it was a tiny little resort that you could rent out for your friends and family.

Upon our return, Danny and I were looking through an international real estate magazine and guess what we saw? The little adorable resort on Shingle Cove was for sale! I called the number and spoke to the owner and grilled them about the property and spoke to the Scottish property manager to gather as much info as I could.

We decided to go down and check the place out before we made an offer.

Who in the world would have thought that, just a few short years earlier, we would be trying to pay off massive legal debt, and now we were actually buying a vacation home? And since it was already an up-and-running rental, we decided to keep the staff in place as it was.

We loved our little piece of paradise and took pride in bringing our friends and family to enjoy the place whenever possible. Many happy cocktail parties were had as the sun went down over the ocean.

The first year we owned Shingle Cove, things went by relatively without incident. The second year, we started having a few problems with petty theft. Sometime thereafter, a tiny little hut bar was built right above our place, and it wasn't exactly attracting the best type of crowd.

We started getting a lot of complaints about the noise from the bar and we started to have more problems with thefts. The only choice we had at that point was to build security bars over all the doors and windows and instructed our guests that they should lock everything when they went to bed for the evening. We even hired security at night, but we could not stop the crime.

Locals were coming down with machetes and trying to rob our guests. It turned out that because our place was so secluded, we were getting targeted by a gang. I spent days on the phone trying to get assistance from the prime minister's office and the tourist board. *Anyone* who might be able to help. Finally, they caught the thieves and our crime spree had ended, but it had soured us to owning our little piece of heaven.

We didn't have any more problems after this, but neither of us wanted the liability. So, you might want to think twice before buying in a foreign country. That's all I'm saying!

DETROIT

1996

INTERESTINGLY ENOUGH, WITH DETROIT'S reputation as a troubled city, I knew I needed to be vigilant about keeping a close eye on Danny. It seemed there could be a lot of trouble to be had in the Motor City. For whatever reason, this period turned out to be our least tumultuous.

I think maybe being a new father put the brakes on Danny's bad behavior. Or perhaps I was just so busy with a two-year-old that I didn't have time to notice if he was up to no good. Either way, I could not have guessed what tumult lay ahead, though it was great to have a brief break from the madness and fast pace of our life in Chicago. Danny would do his morning show on 95.5 and come home and fish or take Isabella to the park. I had put Isabella in preschool two half days a week as I wanted to socialize her with other children. She was such a joy, a happy and affectionate little girl. She did inherit her father's temper, though. Watch out if the Countess does not get her way. But she was too young to realize that she was up against my will.

We packed up the SUV and headed east. At least now Maxi had a little more room than in the infamous Camaro featured in the high-speed reckless endangerment/prostitute incident in Phoenix.

I wasn't that busy as Danny's manager because there wasn't a real showbiz career happening at that time.

We did find a charming little house in West Bloomfield on Walnut Lake. Danny did mornings in 1996.

He would work and come home, and we would take our little boat out on the lake to fish and play on the lakeshore. In the winter, we played in the snow and made a lot of fires in the fireplace and forts with all the furniture on the living room floor.

One of my favorite things about living in Detroit was that my dear friend Jackie Kallen lived there as well. Jackie is one of the most badass women I have ever known. They call her the first woman of boxing. She was the first woman that the boxing community took seriously as a female manager. She managed James "Lights Out" Toney and Leon Spinks, to name a few. They actually made a film about her called *Against the Ropes*, starring Meg Ryan in the role of Jackie. The weird thing was, in the movie Jackie had no kids and wasn't married, as she was in real life. Though right after I moved to Detroit she started going through a very painful breakup with her husband. I thought her real existence was far more interesting than the movie version turned out to be.

She has always been a mentor to me and it was wonderful to spend so much time with her. One time we were at lunch and her phone rang. She took the call and when she got off, she said. "So that was Bob."

"Bob?" I inquired.

"Yes, my friend Bob would like us to come to his show in Ann Arbor."

"Okay. Bob who?"

"Dylan. Wanna go?"

"Do I want to go see Bob Dylan? Is that a trick question?"

Another time, Danny and I rented an RV and drove through the thousand chain lakes in Canada and back through Niagara Falls. Our daughter loved it so much. We definitely didn't know what we were doing and were yelled at in almost every campground we pulled into.

"Your water hose is hooked up wrong."

"You're leaking water all over the campground!"

"You can't dump your waste like that!"

We weren't the most seasoned of campers.

While out driving one day, we came across a wild animal park. They warned us not to drive an RV through, as apparently it would drive the monkeys wild. The thing about Danny is if you said "don't do it," he'd only hear two words: "do" and "it." Almost immediately the monkeys started swarming the RV. They were pulling everything off they possibly could. Then, to top it off, they decided to sit on the front of the RV hood and masturbate toward the window.

"Mommy, what're the monkeys doing?"

"Oh nothing, Isabella."

Danny and I were laughing so hard we were crying.

So, just some advice: don't drive your RV through. Apparently it makes them very, very horny.

Isabella would have been a happy girl had we been able to live in the RV. As we pulled into our driveway to unload, she kept yelling, "More camping, Mommy and Daddy...more!" Unfortunately, vacation had ended and we had to return to the real world. Danny returned back to work, and a few months later we received some great news.

And then New York City called. They wanted to move Danny to mornings on Big105. I was elated, and so proud of Danny—he was hitting the number one market in the USA!

GO AHEAD, BITE THE BIG APPLE

1998

I'VE BEEN FASCINATED BY New York since high school. My choir teacher in Hixson thought it wise to take fifty of us country bumpkins to the Big Apple to experience the cream of the crop in the world of art, fashion, and stage. We certainly were not exposed to this caliber of performances in Chattanooga.

Sometimes we'd get the odd rock show here and there: Rick Springfield, The Go Go's, Billy Squire. But all the big acts were usually in Atlanta or Nashville. We loaded into the bus and drove the fourteen hours. As we drove through the Holland tunnel, the excitement in the bus mounted. We were spending six nights in the city. Each day and night was packed with Broadway shows, concerts, and museums.

All our free time was mostly spent trying to sneak into the bars at night. At the time, the drinking age was eighteen; most of us on the trip were between sixteen and eighteen years old. We stayed at a hotel across the street from the Met on the Upper East Side.

We spent our time at the hotel making mischief and acting as uncultured as one would imagine fifty teenagers from the South without their parents' supervision could manage. One bar down the street called the Monk's Inn looked unassuming. You had to walk down a flight of steps and it was rather dark, so there were no windows for some nosey cop to look into and come down and demand our IDs. Having just returned from the opera *La Traviata*, we were all dressed up in our finest attire. We befriended the bartender there and pretty much landed at the Monk's Inn every night because he would serve us. To say we were having the time of our young lives would be an insult to the phrase. We were having a *mondo* unbelievable magical time!

The last night we were there, we invited the very cute bartender to come and hang out at our hotel in our room.

When he got off work, he showed up with his very weird friend. This sophisticated older gentleman (I'm thinking mid-twenties) mesmerized me with stories about CBGB, Max's Kansas City, and places I had never heard of. He wanted to take me there. This was 1981. I wasn't tuned into girls getting kidnapped and murdered, but at least I had the sense to stay put. (For purposes of this book…damn, I wish I would have gone! Opportunity to live/great story to tell. I'm thinking toss-up.)

Then the cute bartender took me in another room. I couldn't even get a date at Hixson High, jeez—I had to go all the way to NYC to get attention from a man.

Then things started to turn a little nutty. He asked me if I had ever seen a naked man before. I had not, and I was not that interested in seeing one now either. But he was quite insistent that I see one, and it should be him.

He dropped his pants. Yikes! That was way more than I had bargained for. It was time to invite naked man and his weird friend to leave. As I left the room, his friend began throwing up rice soup all over the other bed. They had become rather offended that we told them to go, and as they left the hotel they tried to vandalize as much as possible on their way out the door.

Our teacher caught wind of this story from the management, and the only reason we weren't severely reprimanded was she couldn't prove they were in our room. She knew, though. She knew. There were two rooms full of girls. One was a Goody Two-Shoes room of well-behaved girls, and then there was the room I was in. Even the next year when we went back (and I was damn lucky she let me), the last day of that trip, she cornered me on the bus. "Gretchen Hillmer! Everything that has gone wrong on this trip you've had something to do with. You are vice president of this choir and are supposed to be setting a good example for the underclassmen." That was all true unfortunately. I may have set a good example for inmates, but not so much for my fellow students.

Some seventeen years later, I was very, very happy to be returning to the scene of the crime. Danny finished his shift in Detroit at 10:00 a.m., and we were on a flight by 3:00 p.m. Unfortunately, this time our beloved Maxi Priest would not be going with us. We thought it unfair to coop up our Great Dane in a tiny apartment. Our dear friends Kevin and Barb from Chicago had five acres in the suburbs and offered to take him. I'll always be grateful to them that Maxi's last years were spent playing in the yard with other furry friends.

Danny's radio station put us up in an apartment on the Upper East Side while we looked for a permanent place to buy. We were walking distance from Central Park. As soon as we got settled in, we wrapped up in warm clothes and took a walk to the neighborhood grocer. As we left the store and were crossing, Isabella stepped off the curb and into the street. A car was barreling around the corner. Danny threw down his bags of groceries and jumped between the car and Isabella. It was a reminder that we had moved to a place where we had better pay attention at all times. I had nightmares about it for weeks. I never ever let Isabella get more than a foot away from me ever again.

We looked all over the city, but I was particularly interested at looking at this townhouse in the Meatpacking District, in the West Village at the corner of Washington and Christopher streets. It was still the Meatpacking District, so it could be a little dicey. I didn't care. It was the most room for the money and even had a tiny little backyard.

I insisted to Danny that we buy it. It was by far the best investment, in my opinion. Danny finally relented and put a bid in.

We got it.

We were lucky to get Isabella into Our Lady of Pompeii Catholic School. I would walk her down Christopher Street to school every morning. The drag queens would come running out of their shops with toys for her.

We ate out so much because it was just cheaper than buying groceries. You could eat breakfast for $2.99, and our neighborhood had the coolest restaurants. I was living the *Sex in the City* life before Carrie, Samantha, and the rest of the girls.

We talked about getting Isabella an agent and found a great one to rep her. I spent a lot of time taking Isabella to auditions with screaming four-year-olds. She looked so adorable, and she booked many commercials while we lived there.

Another great thing about NYC is the airports. You can get anywhere out of JFK, Newark, or LaGuardia. Danny had been doing a lot of work in Australia. When his *Esquire* article ran, we went there for two weeks and he did stand-up in Sydney and Melbourne. Off of that, he was offered a job hosting *Tonight Live with Steve Vizard* in Sydney. Then, he had an offer to cohost a radio show in Australia via ISDN line. In exchange for that, they were willing to give us a first-class trip anywhere in the world. We had been so fortunate to expose our daughter to many countries.

By the time Isabella was ten, she had been to St. Lucia, Turks and Caicos, Mexico, England, and Japan.

We chose to go to Bali.

We took Eva Airlines to Taiwan and stayed overnight at the Palace Hotel. The funny thing was they thought I was the famous one, as they kept insisting I was Kyra Sedgwick. I told them I wasn't, but they believed I was. I am quite sure Kevin Bacon would have wanted to know what the hell Kyra was doing in Taiwan with Danny Partridge.

We woke up the next day and caught our connection to Denpasar. They were putting us up at the Four Seasons. The smell of frangipani was so thick in the air. I'll never forget the way Bali smelled: lemongrass and cempaka incense thick in the air. It was definitely one of the most different and interesting countries I had ever experienced. There were rice paddy fields everywhere and little temples on every corner with offerings to the gods. We were there over two major festivals—the culmination of Ramadan and the moon goddess festival or something like that—so there were little gatherings all over the city.

We took Isabella to ride elephants. I am in love with elephants! Their eyes are so expressive, and I love how elephants mourn their dead. When you are immersing yourself in another's country, they aren't interested in your American attitude. The guy who was driving the elephant had this little hammer and was hitting the elephant's head to get it to go where he wanted. I started freaking out and yelling at the guy. He kept telling me it didn't hurt the elephant and I was like, well, why does he have little cuts on his head? Please don't do that while I'm on this elephant again, I begged. I'm sure he was happy to get me off his elephant. I think about that elephant all the time and hope he's okay and has some kind of decent quality of life.

When Isabella was in first grade, because of my love of the Brownies and Girl Scouts, I took the course to become a Girl Scout leader. Don't laugh! I *loved* being a Girl Scout and camping at Camp Potawatomie Hills when I was a kid. For one thing, we were able to pick a camp nickname that we wanted to go by. I was happy to be rid of the name Gretchen for the week. One year I was Rocky and another Bambi, which totally sound like stripper names to me now. What's up with that?

I would count the days at the end of each session when I could go back again the following year. I felt so grown up, being away from my parents, staying in a cabin or tent with five other girls. We would talk about everything. Boys, TV shows and movies we liked, who our favorite counselor was.

And we'd laugh all the time. Like when we sat down to eat our lunch after a hike and I made the unfortunate choice of sitting on top of a hornet's nest. I don't think I could ever explain to you how painful it was to have about fifty hornet stings on your rear end. I also don't think the girl sitting next to me was all that pleased by this either.

We swam in the lake, canoed, learned silly songs, learned arts and crafts. I'm sure my parents had their fill of dream catchers and potholders.

At the end of each session, we'd have a talent show. Naturally, being the showoff that I was, I tried hard to win the spot to represent our group.

We had to make up an act of some kind, and of course mine always included singing. I'm not sure if I always won the spot because of pure talent, or if I was just the most obnoxious about it so they always elected me. I guess I knew then that I wanted a life in show business, though what I eventually got wasn't exactly what I was thinking about then.

Now, as one of Isabella's troop leaders, I loved helping the girls achieve their patches. I do wonder why they deemed me the best choice to head up the cookie sales one year. I don't think putting someone who flunked applied math so many times should have been in charge of the money and accounting. I bet the books were totally messed up at the end of cookie season. Danny let Isabella go on the air and ask his listeners to buy a box or two. I think Isabella smashed the record that year for most boxes sold.

Danny's radio show was super hooked up with all things New York. We were very fortunate to get tickets for every great show. Especially during the holidays. I was very lucky to bring my family to Radio City Music Hall and the Broadway version of *Scrooge* because Danny's radio station was able to help me get good rates on tickets. It made me feel good that my family, who had stuck by Danny through thick and thin, got to enjoy some of the good times and that we got to say thank you in a small way.

We must have seen every Broadway production that was running during that time period. I would have to say the happiest I was, was living in Manhattan. I never felt more myself.

I will always, *always* cherish the time that I spent there. But all good things must come to an end.

Which happened when they wanted Danny to move to Los Angeles.

WELCOME TO LOS ADULTERY

May 1998

DANNY JUST WASN'T ABLE to crack NYC. At that time, Howard Stern was king of terrestrial radio. He was unbeatable. Even though Danny's ratings were okay, they decided to switch formats—to a Spanish-speaking format, if I remember. *No bueno* for Danny.

I was *so* distraught about moving. I loved NYC and hoped we would be there forever.

While we were in NYC, Danny was getting a lot of TV work out of LA. He appeared on *That '70s Show* and a bunch of other smaller gigs. The countdown for us to transplant yet again was on.

We bided our time while Danny's contract was renegotiated. With no job to go to in NYC, we tried to make our last weeks in the city count, taking Isabella to the Central Park Zoo, museums, and other sites, trying to soak up every last ounce of culture.

We decided the one thing we were missing was a doggie. One afternoon, after Danny and I had been having afternoon cocktails, we walked by a pet store called Urban Pets. A huge crowd stood in front of the window. What in the world could be so interesting? Danny and I pushed through the crowd to see the strangest, funniest-looking dog we had ever seen. Danny barged into the store, demanding they take this creature out of the window. They put this pathetic-looking dog on Danny's lap. He was in love! This little hairless puppy, jumping all over us, licking our faces and going absolutely nuts. Apparently this dog had a whole wardrobe, too. After all, this was the West Village.

Danny pleaded, "Pleeeaase, can we have him?"

We took the dog—sailor hats, fur hats, fur coats and all. We went to pick up Isabella from school and she was also in on the lovefest for this dog! We took him home and decided to name him Sid Vicious Bonaduce. Every day when I went to pick up Isabella from school, I dressed him—S—in his fur coat and hat and put him in the stroller.

As I walked through the village, people approached to see my baby—and then recoiled, asking if I was aware my "baby" was a dog. People thought I had gone nuts. Siddy would become a major part of our lives for the next fourteen years. Siddy was like a cat in that he had nine lives. He was the Rasputin of doggies. (He survived a coyote attack, licking bug poison off his feet, AND being run over by a car...this dog did not want to leave his mommy.) It took a vet, when he was fifteen years old, to convince me I wasn't doing Sid any favors by keeping him around. He was blind and had dementia and just barked and barked until he found me in the house. Such a hard day to put an animal down.

We finally got the orders for Danny to start at Star 98.7 in Los Angeles. I loved the music on this station and was excited about that. The day we moved was rainy and chaotic, which turned out to be good for me. Everything was going wrong and I didn't have time to think about the fact that it was my last day in New York.

As soon as the movers let me know they were finished, I gathered up Isabella and Sid (who I had to smuggle in my coat) and headed for the hotel. Our flight was leaving in the morning. I watched the rain out my hotel window and tried not to weep.

The next day we boarded our flight to LA with Siddy in the doggie baggage. I pushed him under the seat and sat down and buckled my seat belt. I just closed my eyes and a thought came over me... This fucking town was going to ruin my marriage. Boy oh boy, did I hit the nail on the head.

Spring 1999

WE ARRIVED ON A beautiful, crisp April day. Danny had put a bid on a home that we were waiting to close on. In the meantime, we would stay with his mother, Betty—in the Valley. Danny had found an amazing house in the Hollywood Hills: four stories, built on a cliff, with an elevator. He had called me about it but was unsure if he should buy it. I said, "Honey, if you love it, I don't need to see it." I wanted him to have his dream California home, as he was back where his entire adult life was trying so hard to return to. That was a quality about Danny that I hated: he had a terrible time enjoying the moment and was constantly in fear about the future.

I guess with his addict behavior I could see why he was always afraid of the future. He was excited about starting his new radio show, though.

Now that we were deeply entrenched in the LA showbiz hustle, Danny started to get a lot of work doing news shows like *Bill Maher* and CNN. He became the go-to guy when any Hollywood folks got into trouble.

And if this doesn't tell you how much Danny had cleaned up his reputation, a new male version of *The View* was casting. Danny went into the audition and nailed it! The cast would include Dick Clark, Mario Lopez, and Dr. Jan Adams (who would be in trouble a few years later for doing plastic surgery on Kanye West's mother). I could not believe that we had come this far. Being an ex-child star joke to cohosting *The Other Half.* That's the thing about America. America loves a good comeback. And his being a cherished child star from an iconic show, people rooted for Danny. I certainly was grateful that people were so forgiving.

To celebrate his comeback, we decided to take a diving trip to Tahiti. Because of Danny's success, we were able to invite his best friend and his best friend's sister on the trip, too. We planned this elaborate cruise to Tahiti, Bora Bora, Raiatea, and Mo'orea.

I was buying some cute bathing suits and outfits to take on the trip when I noticed things were getting snug around my belly. Since it is unsafe to dive if you are pregnant, I figured I better take a pregnancy test in case.

I came home and took the test. Turned out Isabella would be getting a brother or sister.

I was elated that God would bless us with two children. A few weeks later, we left for our trip. I couldn't believe that I wasn't getting sick. I had been very ill with morning sickness and terrible acid reflux with Isabella. It looked like I was going to dodge that the second time around.

And then the second night of the trip I was getting dressed for dinner and it hit me out of nowhere. Insane amounts of vomit. I got into bed and told Danny that I wouldn't be able to make it to dinner. He offered to get me food. The sweetheart came back with a tray of food and the first thing I saw? Pea soup.

I started heaving at the site of it.

Guys, when your pregnant wife needs food, bringing something that resembles vomit is a very bad idea! I tried to suck it up the best I could on that trip. A rocking boat wasn't the best choice, but Polynesia was such an unbelievably lovely place. I can't wait to go back one day when I'm not blowing chunks. When we returned from our lovely trip, I went to the doctor to have an ultrasound. We would be having a son this time.

Perfect. My boy and my girl.

I was able to track down Kristine Davis, a supervising producer for a TV show called *A Baby Story*. She was such a wonderful lady and I looked forward to working with her on this show. A few years later she would hire me as an associate producer for another show she was on called *Life Moments* (side note...which interestingly enough would end up replacing *The Other Half* a year later when it was cancelled).

We started shooting when I was about seven months pregnant.

I cannot tell all of you how grateful I was to have that documentation of our son's birth. That show always makes me cry. Count Dante Jean Michael Valentino Bonaduce was born at Cedar Sinai Hospital on February 14, 2001—an apropos date for the sweetest child in the world to be born. Not only was Dante a super loving child but he also looked like a cherub. People would stop me all the time and comment on his angelic face. He also inherited his dad's sense of humor.

My favorite story of all time about Dante goes like this:

When Dante first started talking, he used to walk up to guys and pull on their pants leg and ask them:

"'Scuze me, mister...do you have tiny balls?"

The guy would look at me and ask, "Lady. Did your kid just ask me if I have tiny balls?"

"Yes, yes he did," I'd answer with a straight face. "He wants a marble and he thinks all people carry them in their pockets."

Ha! Have you ever seen that Dave Matthews video where the guy was walking down the street and randomly hugging people? That was like Dante. The grocery store lady would check us out, he'd run around and hug her, our waiter would bring our food, he'd jump up and hug him, the dry-clean guy would bring me my clothes, and yep—you guessed it—Dante would hug him. I hated that the day came when I had to tell him he couldn't do that anymore. It was freaking people out. That's what kind of society we live in. It's not like I had to say, "Dante, you can't wave that gun around." I had to tell a child to stop hugging people. How sad is that?

***

BEFORE OUR MARRIAGE WENT to hell, we took the kids on trips and tried to be a real family. Like the time we rented an RV and drove the kids out with us to Phoenix. At my insistence, we drove like a bat out of hell to get to the Mining Camp before it closed for the night and the season. I wanted my children to experience one of my very favorite childhood places to dine.

When I was only five years old and living with my grandparents—during my parents' divorce proceedings—they often took my brother Kurt and me to eat at the Mining Camp in Apache Junction. I loved that place, though it scared me a little, too. Legend had it that gold miners had gone missing looking for the lost treasure of Captain Kidd. While I was afraid, I was also intrigued that I could possibly get killed by Indians while eating my dinner. We'd sit at these huge picnic tables, and the wait staff would bring out all-you-could-eat platters of BBQ, corn on the cob, and biscuits.

Our family trip worked out to be the last day of the Mining Camp's season. En route, we got lost on the dark roads, and I called the restaurant and begged them not to close until we got there. Sweetly, they stayed open to accommodate us. Danny had had about enough of being lost on the dirt roads and was not in the best of moods when we arrived. Two dogs jumping all over us. Kids screaming. I was just chuckling at the madness and knew it would all be great once we arrived.

But I had become one of those super annoying parents that insists her children enjoy the experience as much as she had as a child.

I had joined ranks with those parents that I see at the zoo who keep obnoxiously yelling, "See the monkey? Do you hear the monkey? Look at the monkey!" Why is it as parents we assume our kids have become deaf and blind when we go to the zoo? It takes everything I have not to yell, "They see the fucking monkey! We *all* see the monkey!"

And somehow, I turned this experience into that! After my motley crew and I walked into an empty restaurant and planted ourselves at one of the long tables with the tin plates and cups, I started with the questions and urgings.

"Taste these ribs… Mmm. Yummy! Aren't they good?"

"Oh these, biscuits! Put some jelly on them!"

Everyone was so uptight from the ride that nobody had fun. A do-over is in order soon! We will have to wait, however, as the place burned to the ground in 2016. I'm first in line as soon as it opens.

Spring 2001

WHEN DANNY WAS IN his twenties, he lived on a boat. He always wanted to be in a position to buy another one. The first one he bought was a beautiful sailboat. It was just too much work to take out on the ocean. He spent many drunken weekends on that boat, but for me, being pregnant and uncomfortable, it wasn't the way I wanted to spend my time. I spent many weekends alone at the house while he was down there, and when he realized it was hard to take a sailboat out by yourself, he decided to buy a big motorboat instead.

The only thing was—Danny, fancying himself a pirate, was causing him to have a serious drinking problem. Danny was in such bad shape that I had a friend come over and do an intervention on Danny. With the shape he was in, there was no way he was going to be able to do all this work. We were supposed to take another cruise, but instead of going on our European vacation, we checked Danny into rehab.

We traded off going to the boat on weekends for spending family day with Danny in Malibu. This was his second attempt at rehab, and I was hoping it would take. He would send me lovely letters and I had real hope he was going to once and for all get himself together.

Once he was out, he was very diligent about going to AA meetings. I would try to go with him as much as I could. I went to one Alanon meeting and it just wasn't for me. I felt like it was a lot of people taking responsibility and blaming themselves for other people's drinking problems. I am sure they've helped millions, but I have always felt each person is responsible for what they put in their body. I didn't make him take shots or do drugs. Was I an enabler in some way? Clearly, but I felt I was helping keep Danny alive in whatever manner I needed to do it. I didn't feel like I needed to apologize for that to anyone.

This boat was far more comfortable for me to be on. It had a stateroom, a living room, and a kitchen. It was very nice. Once Dante was born, we spent quite a few weekends on the boat. Danny was about to start shooting *The Other Half* and he was trying to make the most of his free time. Between the radio show Monday through Friday, and taping the TV show a couple of times a week, he was about to get very busy.

They filmed the first season at Sunset Gower Studios. I would try to come down with the kids for the tapings whenever I could manage.

The show was set to debut on September 11, 2001. I don't have to tell you guys what happened on that day. When the show finally did start to air, nobody was interested in new television shows. Somehow, they did well enough to get renewed for the 2002/03 season. That season would be my personal 9/11.

Before the second season started, Dick and Carrie Clark invited us over for a celebration dinner at their Malibu house. I had actually been to his house years before. My roommate from Chicago had briefly dated his son, DeWayne Clark, and he wanted us to fly in from Chicago for his birthday. His dad was out of town, so he snuck us in over there for a little party. I even slept in the guest room.

I decided not to mention this. They had a beautiful sit-down dinner for all of the cast members. I was lucky and got seated next to Dick, so I had a wonderful time chatting with him. I asked him if he was going to be in Times Square again this year to shoot *Dick Clark's New Year's Rockin' Eve*. He was quiet for a moment, and then said, "I'm absolutely terrified, but I have to go." He and Carrie were such lovely people. It charmed me so much that he said his favorite song was Madonna's "Vogue," and he kept playing it over and over that night. We really did lose an American treasure when he passed away. I'll never forget watching him on the TV after his stroke. Cheers to the producers for keeping him on through that.

9021HO

Fall 2002

DANNY WAS GETTING HOME later and later from his show tapings. Around the holidays, 98.7 would do this concert called *Not So Silent Night*. The lineup that year was Moby, Matchbox 20, and Nora Jones, among others. Danny asked me to get some extra tickets for some of his colleagues on *The Other Half*. For most of the concert, Danny was nowhere to be found. I didn't care much because I was having a ball dancing and just listening to all the great music.

In the middle of the show, Danny comes up and says Moby is going bowling with Christina Ricci and wants to know if we want to come. Are you joking? Bowling with Moby? That's like archery with Bon Jovi! We're going!

For some odd reason, Danny was pouting about this. We got to the bowling alley and had a great time with Moby and Christina and her sister.

A few nights later, *The Other Half* had their Christmas party. We went, and after a while this girl walked up to us and was talking to us. When we got into the car to leave, I said to Danny that he and that girl seemed to be having a conversation over my head and I didn't like it. I had caught it and didn't trust my gut. He, of course, as usual, said I was crazy and used his usual deflection tactic.

At the last minute, I had found a cruise for us to go on in Mexico that departed from Long Beach. Danny was not happy about going. He pretty much said to me, if he were to drink on this cruise, he would blame me because I put him on a ship with alcohol.

Something was different about the way he was treating me. He had become incredibly cold to me, and also very vicious. I tried to block it out and have fun with the kids. Of course, he did drink on the cruise, and of course blamed me for it.

The day we got off the boat, we drove home. The minute we got to the house, Danny basically dumped me, the luggage, and the kids out of the car and said, "You made me go on that cruise and now I drank. I need to get away from here for a few days. I'm driving up the coast by myself."

Danny had been such an unbearable cock on that trip; quite frankly, I wasn't sad to see him go. Things went on like this for what felt like forever. Danny would go get coffee at Starbucks and come back an hour and a half later claiming the line was very long.

Things were just not adding up.

One thing I learned at this time was that I had an incredible knack for coming up with great reality show ideas. Fisher Entertainment, which was producing *The Other Half*, even optioned a bunch of show ideas from us.

But then we would be driving to pitch meetings and in the car his phone would ring, and when I answered, they would hang up. Any woman knows this is not a good sign. I would soon find out my worst nightmare was about to come true: in the form of 9021HO. This is the only name I will refer to her by in this entire book, so don't try to get it out of me.

I'll never forget when I confronted him. We were sitting in the backyard at our home, and I just said, "Something's going on here, Danny, and you need to tell me the truth."

He sort of hung his head and blurted it out: "Okay, yes, I'm in love with someone else."

"Whhhhhhaaaattt?" I just started hyperventilating. I knew it. I grabbed his phone and started stomping on it. I kind of blacked out for a second, but it is quite possible I started to attack him AND his phone. I was going absolutely sideways over this. "Where does she live?" I shouted. "I said, where does she live?"

He was silent and finally said, "Down the street." He grabbed his phone away from me before I could throw it in the pool. I guess he had moved her right down the street for easier access.

I was livid and ordered him out. As he went to pack his stuff, I found his phone and her number.

I looked up the number for Gloria Allred's office and programmed her phone number in under 9021HO. That way, every time Danny tried to call that ho, he'd be reminded what he was risking.

When I found out he had been cheating, I was so afraid of a sexual harassment suit that I made him go and get every single piece of correspondence, every picture, *anything*, and bring it back to our house because I just wanted to have evidence that this was a consensual situation.

Now things were starting to make sense. He was delivering her steaming hot Starbucks coffee and delivering me my cold non-frothy beverage. My ProFlowers that he was getting in exchange for doing their ads were getting swiped off the porch so he could bring them to Ho.

Well, it took him about twenty-four hours to realize he might be making a mistake and returned to plead with me to forgive him. This was topped off by Ho calling me and leaving me messages about how Danny would be a better man with her. And how God would be okay with their affair.

Oh really? Is that the eleventh commandment? "Disregard that thing about how thou shall not commit adultery."

Right before I found out this lovely news, I was doing a fundraiser for the Camp Pendleton wives. First, they had their military ball, and most of the wives can barely afford diapers, let alone a gown. In Hollywood, you can only wear your gown once, so I collected a bunch of gowns and sent them down to them so they would have dresses.

The second thing I did was collect Easter baskets. (What's with me and Easter disasters? First my wedding, now this!)

Danny was very insistent that if we drove down, he had to attend an AA meeting while we were there. I picked a hotel without a bar and asked about the closest AA meeting. We had to collect a couple hundred baskets for the kids. I was elated with the Star 98.7 listeners and the sponsor, Peter Fice, for making this happen.

As we drove down the day before, Danny viciously tore into me.

"Why the fuck do I have to be here?" he screamed at me. "What the hell do you do?" he asked, dripping with sarcasm. "Do you read books? Do you take a class?" Apparently, he and this Ho would read books to each other (so did we, in the beginning) and take classes together.

"Oh, I don't know, Danny. Let's see, I fucking take care of our kids and our business, since you don't help!"

That didn't seem to faze him. He berated me all the way there, and then when we couldn't find the AA meeting, he really went crazy. I later realized the reason he was being so mean: Saturday nights were apparently their nights to be together, and I was forcing him to come with me to deliver the baskets.

I don't know whether she put the pressure on him when I made him do something with me, or if he just resented that he had to be with me and would get mad about it.

Danny had told me there was an AA meeting on Sunday mornings at seven. He said that he would never be able to make it in time from our house and said he needed to stay on the boat. Of course I wanted to support his sobriety, and I agreed it was a good idea, never thinking he was staying with her on the boat on Saturdays.

I don't even know why I wanted to work things out.

Wait I know why. When I made him get the letters they had written to each other, she mentioned many times about being stepmother to our children and picking them up from school.

Oh, no you won't, bitch!

Over my dead body would that women would be stepmother to our children.

And there you have it, folks. Your answer as to why I didn't kick him to the curb sooner. I was in the very weird position of being married to a man when I was also his manager, his publicist, completely involved with trying to keep him out of trouble, his business partner, his children's mother, *everything*. I made him give me all the correspondence and then I said to him, "You are going to see how bad you hurt me, because you're going to sit there and I'm going to read every one of these things in front of you. And you're going to see by the look on my face how much you just crushed me."

But I have to say if I had to pick the one thing that was by far the worst offense, it would be when Danny came home one day from work. He walked in and said to me, "I have a surprise for you."

I could not guess what it was.

He pulled out his hand from behind his back and showed me his ring finger. He had gone to a tattoo artist and had a wedding ring tattooed on his finger. He proudly stated that he had done that for me. Danny was always doing grand gestures. I thought it was sweet, but because of how bad things had been with us it seemed like strange timing.

And it was.

It actually was for HER; she had a matching one.

The next day on Danny's TV show, he proudly showed off his ring tattoo and proclaimed how he had done that for his wife that he loved so much. The audience, of course, went crazy. Danny had once again racked up points for being "such a romantic guy, who obviously loved his wife so much!" How could somebody stoop that low?

Amongst all the stuff, I found a poem he had written her—some hokey, stupid poem about how all the balloons are beautiful but the blue balloons are the most beautiful balloons of all. Later that week I was driving along Los Feliz Boulevard past her apartment and I saw a bunch of blue balloons flying from her balcony. *Why you Smart Alec little...*

This bitch had blue balloons and has tied them to her balcony and I know exactly what she was trying to say: "*I'm* the blue balloon; *I'm* the one you want!"

I got my neighbor, Julie Campbell, to dress up as a gardener with me and try to help me get those balloons down. I have never loved a woman more. It was a caper of *I Love Lucy* proportions, and she was the Ethel to my Lucy.

We dressed up like two gardeners and brought a huge hook with us because 9021HO's apartment was on the third story. We drove there and waited for the gate to open as someone was leaving and then drove into the garage and parked. We found our way out of the garage and we were standing under the balcony, two women dressed in gardener's clothes, with large straw hats on our heads, trying to maneuver a hook on an enormously long pole to bring the balloons down. Unfortunately, the hook wasn't long enough to reach. To make matters worse, when we tried to leave, we couldn't get out of the garage! We were stuck in 9021HO's garage dressed up like gardeners wearing big straw hats, trying to open the door of every single car to find a gate opener so we could get the hell out of there before we got caught. After setting off car alarms left and right, we finally found a car that was unlocked *and* had a gate opener, and we made our escape.

And, of course, LA rewards bad behavior. I turn on my TV periodically and see her face. She had her own show. I bust my rear in this town and try to do it ethically, and someone like her has her own show.

Thanks for having my back, Los Angeles. Really appreciate it!

MOMMY FLEW OVER
THE CUCKOO'S NEST

GOD HAVE MERCY ON ME AND LET ME FORGET THIS DATE. FOREVER.

Danny's radio station held contests in which they'd fly listeners to anywhere in the world that a big rock band was playing, huge musicians like the Rolling Stones and David Bowie. The listeners called in to the radio station and if they were picked, would win two tickets for airfare, their hotel room, and tickets to the show. We would all fly together in the same plane to wherever the concert was. In this particular instance, the Rolling Stones were playing in Amsterdam, so Danny and I decided to go too since we had never been there.

I was a little worried, however. The first rehab Danny had been to diagnosed his number one problem as sex addiction. According to Danny, they claimed that treatment for drugs and alcohol was not going to work if they didn't also treat him for that. Lo and behold, Amsterdam is quite famous for its Red Light District in De Wallen—the streets lined with shops, in the windows of which are women, men, trans people, you name it, dressed in S&M outfits, cheap lingerie, feathers, fetish attire, and almost anything else you can imagine.

At Christmas time, when I was little, we would go and look at the window displays in downtown Chicago. Every store would try to outdo the next with the most elaborate holiday displays. This was kind of like that—only the porn equivalent.

I couldn't help wondering where these people came from and what kind of lives they'd had before they ended up here. As we walked down the street, we came upon a place that had live sex shows. I started to get a very sick feeling in my stomach because I knew Danny would want to go into one of those places. My friend Bill Hicks used to do a funny bit about not wanting to see his own hairy bob'n man ass and that he certainly did not want to see someone else's, either. I felt exactly the same way.

I was afraid to go in and even more afraid to let Danny go in alone, because I wasn't sure what he could come out with—both figuratively and literally!—and so I mustered up all the courage that I could and I followed him inside. It was dark and very loud. There were rows and rows of benches and tables where people were sitting drinking and waiting for the show.

All of a sudden, the theme song from *Phantom of the Opera* started blaring out of the speakers. A girl dressed as the female lead, Christine, from the Broadway play, sexily walked onto the stage. Then a man dressed as the Phantom of the Opera, complete with the famous mask, followed her out. They started reenacting some sort of porn version of the play. If it weren't so disgusting it would've been hilarious. Thank God Danny lost interest pretty quickly, and we left.

Of course, the first place Danny and every other person on that plane wanted to go to were the drug cafés. Back in 2003, you could go to little cafés where you could buy mushrooms, pot, and the like.

I don't do drugs, I don't like drugs, and most of my drug use was smoking pot when I was thirteen years old—with the exception of *one* time, to prove a point to Danny I did not like drugs, that I agreed to smoke part of a joint. Since my system was so clean, I became incredibly high and paranoid, *so* high that I thought two funny-looking guys in braids had just run through my apartment. Apparently there had been a commercial on TV with that exact theme, but Danny was laughing so hard at my freak-out that he could not assure me I *had* actually seen that, albeit on TV. Needless to say, that was the last of my drug experimentation. I didn't want to go to the drug café, but I *did* want to experience Amsterdam because, you know, it's a different society with different rules. Because it was legal there, it didn't seem like I was breaking the law, which I would never have done in the United States. I didn't even know what everybody was buying; they were just ordering from the café menu and getting high.

Eventually we ended up back at the bar in the hotel and we met two guys who seemed like very nice chaps. After a few minutes of conversation, I realized that these Dutch guys were drug dealers; they sit at the bar of the hotel and sell drugs to tourists, the kind of drugs you can't buy in the cafés. Well, when in Rome, right? Or Amsterdam, anyway.

I dove right into a deep conversation with the drug dealers. At this point, drinks were aplenty. I mean *a lot* of alcohol was being consumed, everybody was on drugs except for me and also extremely drunk. I was sitting at the bar talking to one of them, who I found out was a painter and who was very interesting. He was a painter/drug dealer, which was *fascinating* to me because, of course, I love the baddest boy I can find in the room! (I know what you're thinking: How could anyone beat Danny as the baddest boy in the room?) With my bad-boy radar, I found him; *of course* I'm going to talk to him!

There we were, sitting at the bar talking, and all of a sudden Danny came over and sat down, looked at the guy, and said, "So, this is my wife, and my girlfriend lives just down the street from us, and all I want to do is fuck her!"

I broke down crying, devastated and so embarrassed. I couldn't believe Danny just said that to a complete stranger in Holland! This painter guy and I had hit it off and we had been talking for a while. He looked at Danny and said, "Oh my God! I just met this woman, she's an angel! Why would you treat her that way?"

At that point there were fifty or so drinks on the table and I just grabbed one and downed it. Earlier Danny had thought it would be funny to put ecstasy in a drink, but I had caught him in the act out of the corner of my eye. I would never, ever, *ever* take a drug willingly, but I was drunk and crying and I lost track of what drink had the ecstasy in it—and that was the one I accidentally downed. Pretty soon I was really screwed up on ecstasy and sitting there getting agitated; I wasn't having the warm and fuzzy experience that I'd heard one has on ecstasy. Not at all.

I was getting super agitated and really hot. I suddenly felt sick and I wanted to get to the hotel room because I knew I was going to throw up. I somehow got into the elevator, and then I started vomiting all over the place. I was so embarrassed because I couldn't tell the people at the reception desk what was happening to me. They had seen me get into the elevator and I knew they were going to think I was just some drunken, drugged-out American woman. I was so humiliated! I couldn't even tell them that someone had put something in my drink, that it wasn't my fault I was throwing up all over the hotel elevator. So now I was drunk, throwing up, on drugs, and thinking, "Please, God, let me start my period in these white pants so my embarrassment can be complete." Thankfully God, in his infinite mercy, decided to spare me that one.

I called the airline and found out there was a 6:00 a.m. flight back to Los Angeles. I'm going! I'm leaving Danny's ass in Amsterdam to figure out how to get home by himself. I tried to get away, but he saw me waiting for the taxi, so he grabbed his passport and his things and got on the plane, too.

Then he promptly passed out in his first-class seat on God knows what. I did not say one word to him the entire flight back. It's impossible to have a conversation with a passed-out guy, trust me. I was still so ill, agitated, and dehydrated, and now I had to fly for thirteen hours on that plane back to LA with him on the same flight as me.

We got back to Los Angeles and I did what any woman would have done: I threatened to divorce Danny. Did I follow through? Hell no! This was not quite enough humiliation for me; I guess I needed more. The story I am about to tell you…well, my therapist informed me I was clearly having a psychotic break, and you will see why he thought so as the rest of the story unfolds. This was how screwed up my mind was at the time: *I felt like I had to reach out to this Dutch painter/drug dealer to clear my good name with him!* I was convinced Danny had embarrassed *me* by what he said to the guy at the bar and I wanted him to know I really *was* an angel and a great person and he had not been wrong about his assessment of me. And my solution was to go back to Amsterdam and have sex with him.

At this point I was so angry with Danny, I said, "You know what? All I do is worry about where you are and what you're doing and you know what? It's going to be your turn. I'm going to fly back to Amsterdam first class and I'm going to have sex with that guy just to give it back to you—and you're going to pay for it all!"

I bought two first-class tickets to Amsterdam and took my gay friend, Darren Highsmith, because you usually need your gay friend for backup when you're going to do something really bad. We got on the plane and we were so excited (especially him, because he just scored a first-class trip to Europe) and then I decided to call the Dutch guy from the plane to tell him, "Hey, I'm coming back and I would like to get together with you." At this point, we were at least eight drinks in and probably somewhere over Greenland, and I was pretty drunk and yelling on the phone to the Dutch guy, "Oh my God, I'm crazy! I'm crazy! I can't believe I'm coming back there! This is crazy! I'm a lunatic!"

Darren said, "Oh my god! Hang up the phone! Everyone on this plane thinks you're crazy!"

"Why would they think that?"

"Because you keep yelling you're crazy and a lunatic at the top of your lungs."

I decided this was a good time to hang up.

We arrived in Amsterdam and we checked into another nice hotel. We made plans to meet for dinner with the painter/drug dealer. We went over to the hotel and were sitting waiting for him, and when he showed up, he was totally pink! The color of his face was pink! I was thinking to myself, "I didn't notice you were a pink man when I was talking to you…" The first thing he said after he sat down was, "I am scared of you." I asked why, and he said, "Because you kept telling me on the phone that you are a crazy lunatic!" Well, excuse me, I don't speak freaky-deeky Dutch! Now, on top of everything else, I've made this guy *afraid* of me. About ten minutes later, his date showed up. He was so scared of me, he brought a date for protection! I started crying, because I was humiliated in front of this guy yet *again*.

This is how God protects me from myself sometimes. I just don't do bad things and when I try, I think God says "Oh no, no, no. You're not to do something bad in your marriage and I am not going to start letting you do it now. First you're going to call him from the plane and insist that you're crazy and scare the crap out of him and then, when you get there, his date's going to show up and fall asleep with her head on your lap." Thank you, God. I really appreciate that you were watching out for me, even if the lesson was to humble me by having me make a jackass out of myself on two continents.

That was pretty much my payback to Danny. Of course, Danny couldn't say anything because of all the cheating he'd done; he *really* couldn't say anything. In a way he was giving me carte blanche, the cheating get-out-of jail-free card, which is pretty bad in itself. He let me fly back to hang out with the painter/drug dealer in Europe. For God's sake, I was his wife! Should I have been offended that he would let me do that? He thought I was going to be with that Dutch guy all night so he sent champagne to the room for us. I just sat there and drank it by myself, crying and contemplating the fact that I was so out of my mind, I'd almost done something awful.

I honestly can't say what either of us was thinking. This had tipped over into unbelievable lunacy on both our parts. Danny being such a jealous man; sending champagne to my room when he thought I was going to be with another man makes absolutely no sense. Guilt because of all he had put me through? Maybe. Could it have been years and years of mistreating me and maybe he was just numb to what was proper anymore? Or perhaps it was his way of telling the Dutch guy that he was giving me his permission, and he was still in control of the situation. I suspect it was most likely the last scenario.

Later, when I talked to my psychiatrist about this, he said I wouldn't have done it even if the Dutch guy had been willing, because my religious upbringing was just so engrained in my mind that you DO NOT CHEAT!

Maybe so, but I wanted to teach Danny a lesson. So many nights I sat up wondering, where is he? What is he doing? I felt like he needed a little taste of his own medicine.

You have to remember my mindset at this time. I had just found out, not too long ago, that Danny was having an affair with a girl he had moved into an apartment just down the street from our house, literally a few blocks away. I couldn't deny that he had moved the girl down the street; there was no more trying to pretend that it wasn't happening. I always felt he was cheating, but I could never catch him, and whenever I would confront him, he would say things like, "You're crazy! I would never, *never* do that to you!" I believed him and thought maybe I *was* crazy because I couldn't believe that, after everything I had done for this man, that was the way he would repay me. That's a mean thing to do to somebody: to make her question her sanity.

BREAKING BONADUCE

2005

SIDE NOTE. I HAD not seen episodes of *Breaking Bonaduce* in so many years. For purposes of this book, I tried to find them online. All I could find were some clips on VH1. My stomach started hurting just reliving that time! Looking back with a fresh perspective—man, were we incredibly mismatched. It is pretty obvious that we had grown as far apart as two people could be. I also noticed in the few clips that my children were acting out in very obnoxious ways. It was a horrible mistake to put them on TV with the subject matter. I would caution people with small children to really think hard before doing that. It definitely was not a good situation to put my daughter into at the very least as she was old enough to comprehend all of the negativity. The best thing I ever did for this family was pull the plug. And that includes Danny.

The *Osbornes* TV show was a huge hit for MTV during the early 2000s. Every single TV station was looking for the own version of *The Osbornes*. I had come up with this idea called *Rock and Roll Dinner Party* that Danny and I set up a pitch for 3 Ball Entertainment and was very excited when they wanted to option it. Part of the show was going to be taping our therapy and working through this affair that my lovely husband thought was a good idea. If it was going to be a reality show, I wanted it to be real. I refused to even talk about the whole mess until the cameras were rolling. I wanted it to be truthful as to what we were going through and not recreate conversations. I wanted people to see the damage they did to their marriage when they chose to have an affair.

Plus, I wanted to send a message to this town: Be careful whose husband you have an affair with because you never know whose wife is going to have a TV show. I never wanted to give this chick any free press, so I didn't want to say her name.

Luckily, 3 Ball loved the idea and pitched it to VH1, which in turn loved the idea and optioned a pilot. The bad thing about a pilot is that many times they don't air on TV. It's hard to get rock stars to be on a show that is unproven and probably didn't pay and was not going to air, most likely.

We ended up getting Terri Nunn from Berlin (whom I just adore), Janice Dickinson, Bobby Trendy, Sam Rubin, some girl from *Survivor*, and a comic. It was a potluck dinner, so everyone had to bring his or her favorite dish.

I remember the *Survivor* girl brought raw lasagna that I almost puked up by accident! It was a lovely evening and the taping went well. I had insisted that Danny buy me a new ring, as I felt the one I had from so many years ago was now tainted. That evening, Danny presented me with a brand-new emerald-and-diamond ring during dinner.

We were hopeful we could get this show picked up. A few weeks later, we received the news that they didn't like the show, but they liked us and wanted to proceed with a show. Be careful what you wish for.

The one change that they wanted to make was the doctor on the show. Dr. Jenn Berman was a friend of mine and I had suggested her. Ultimately, they decided that Danny was such a strong personality that they needed a male doctor because they thought it could appear that he was "beating up on the doctor." They found a doctor they liked named Dr. Gary and we put together some ideas for the show.

As I mentioned, I'd had aspirations to sing in a band since I was fifteen years old. And now especially, I needed to have something of my own to do other than be a wife and mother. So I asked a friend of Danny's, Chris Doohan (the son of the guy who played Scotty on *Star Trek*), if I could join his band, The Mudflapps. The band agreed. We would rehearse every other week and did a variety of music. It was so much fun, and I was so happy to be singing again.

Back to our show: The first show set the tone for the rest of the episodes. Things went so awry in our therapy that the production company decided to just follow us and dumped all other ideas. The first session with Dr. Gary turned incredibly volatile right off the bat. Danny was telling Dr. Gary that because I didn't have much of a sex drive, I had basically forced him into cheating. We definitely disagreed on this point as to the cause of his infidelity. I personally feel like I could have banged him fifty times a day, and he would have cheated anytime the opportunity presented itself. Because of Danny's constant philandering, I was basically shut down sexually.

I do not think it is possible to have a trusting, close sexual relationship when you don't have that to begin with with your partner.

Danny, being the insanely jealous man that he was—*you better not have a past, and if you did, you better not make the mistake of telling him about it*. I was of a totally different mindset. I wanted my husband to share everything with me. I didn't care what he did before me. It made no difference. The past was the past.

When Danny made the point that I had made him do it, my take was that he was getting the relationship he deserved because he was getting sex elsewhere. This was a vicious circle: What came first, the chicken or the egg?

Now on our TV show, it was essentially full-on reality. They didn't need to set up situations to cause controversy. We had that in spades.

Some of the next episodes dealt with his training porn star women and his steroid use. Danny would come home with boxes of steroids with animals on the cover. I did not feel like this would be a great idea to put in his body. Not to mention the violent mood swings that it caused.

In one scene, they showed Danny injecting steroids. I know Danny regretted that a lot, but I truly was of the mind that if we were living it, let it be the truth. The last thing a person who is bipolar needs is something that can cause mood swings. This was not a great combination.

Danny had gotten his trainer's license and would train girls at the gym. In one of the episodes, Danny is seen training a hairdresser and a lesbian porn star. If they were casting girls for him to train, these two would have been the perfect picks for maximum controversy.

Who knew with Danny? Taping this show was far more stressful than I could ever have imagined.

In one of the episodes, Danny broke a ceramic cup on his head. That was followed by him demanding that I tell Dr. Gary I was in love with him. I honestly wasn't sure I was at that time. People would have thought I was insane if I told this man unraveling on TV that I was in love with him, with the way he was acting and the way he was treating me. Nobody could have been in love with someone who behaved like that. With the way he was acting, I wasn't sure I even liked him. No matter how much Danny demanded on the show that I say it, I refused to be told what to say.

When Prince Charles was asked on TV if he was in love with Lady Diana, he said, "I guess," whatever that means. I had a difficult time wrapping my head around that term, too—and I still do.

I believe there is "I have your back through thick and thin" love and "lust" love. I think "in love" is basically lust. Since that's the way I saw things, it was a term impossible for me to say as he had killed my sexual attraction for him. I would not compromise my soul to say something he demanded I say. EVER!

During one of the episodes, my friends threw me a fortieth birthday party. I was so excited to see my friends. Some flew in from Chicago and Tennessee. My friends Jackie Kallen, Adrienne Maloof Nassif, Lisa Foxx, Barb Olson, Rachel, my assistant Jaclyn, Kirsten Lando (who was married to Joe Lando of *Dr. Quinn Medicine Women*) and Julie Campbell (married to Viv Campbell of Def Leppard) all were in attendance.

My wonderful girlfriend Lisa Foxx, who was and still is one of the top DJs in Los Angeles, helped plan the birthday sleepover party at the W Hotel. A consummate pro and very TV savvy, her whole thought process for the birthday party was, "What would be great TV and how can I help my friends to get some exposure?" She was friends with a white witch, who agreed to come and do a goddess ceremony in my honor.

This did not sit well with my best friend since high school, I am guessing, as she was incredibly religious, and I basically never heard from her again after the show aired. I think between the witch and the strippers it was too much for her Christian sensibility. Ordinarily I would not have wanted a witch to do anything for me, but quite frankly the goddess ceremony she did for me was so meaningful with my girlfriends, and there were no freaky undertones to it. It was rather sweet.

Some other friends of Lisa's were a crew of male dancers. She hired them to come and dance and gave them specific instructions they could not be naked. I knew this would be *incredibly* bad for me. I knew Danny was going to go apeshit!

What you didn't see on camera was me begging one of my friends to be me. These dancers would not have known the difference. All of my friends thought I was being silly and that things would be okay. I knew they would not.

Apparently someone who was out with Danny that night told him there were going to be strippers. He became irrational and demanded that he be taken to the W Hotel. Because Danny was drinking heavily, the producers refused to go and took Danny's keys. Danny resorted to flagging down some guy in a car that was driving by and demanding to be brought to the W Hotel.

Thank goodness that, for whatever reason, he never made it. Instead, he resorted to calling and calling my cell phone. Afterward, I grew tired of his nonsense. I just stopped answering. Then he started calling the phone in the hotel room. Finally, I'd had enough. It was getting very late at night and when I did pick up and speak to him, I was not happy about the way he sounded. He was home with my kids, so I decided to leave the hotel and go check on him.

I went back to my house and found Danny passed out on the couch. I poked him, which was the biggest mistake of my life. The camera crew had gone home, so now I'd just disturbed an angry beehive of a man. He started off demanding to know why I didn't leave the party when the strippers showed up. I knew better at this point than to argue with a drunken, steroid-ridden, possibly-on-drugs person. I tried to walk away and just go to bed, but Danny wanted answers and followed me into the bathroom. At this point I was starting to get a little scared of him because he was acting so crazy.

After I was unresponsive to his rage, he grabbed a razor and slashed his wrists.

I grabbed the phone to dial 911 because he was bleeding all over, and I could not gauge how severe the cuts were. He yanked the phone from my hands and smashed it on the floor. I was starting to shake. I was very, very frightened. I didn't know what he would do next. He just kept yelling and telling me he was dying, and it was my fault.

Suddenly I heard a knock at our front door. Danny walked down the stairs. He opened the door and it was the police. My call had gotten through! Even if it's a hang-up call, usually the police show up just in case someone was forcing you to hang up, which was exactly my case. Danny looked at the officers and one of them said to Danny, "Is everything all right in here?"

I rushed down the stairs and started trying to get the officers' attention, shaking my head no. My nightgown had blood all over it from Danny's wrist cuts. The police officer put his hand on his gun and ordered Danny to move away from me. Several officers were now crowding into my entryway. A female officer escorted me up the stairs and started to question me.

I did my best to stay calm and appear not as frightened as I was. I didn't tell her the whole story because I knew it would be very big trouble for Danny. From downstairs, Danny kept yelling, "Thanks a lot. Thanks. You just ruined my career."

Had he been hip to *Miami Vice* (as I had been all those years ago), he would have known to keep his mouth shut. I guess when you harm yourself, the police consider you a 5150, and you have to stay in a lockdown facility for forty-eight hours. They took him away. I have never ever been so happy to see someone leave in my life.

Once again my parents received the dreaded middle-of-the-night call to come to my rescue. I had to call the production company in the morning to explain what had happened. I was afraid for Danny, yet this time he had gone way, way too far. I'd had it.

Yet, I was still in that very bad place of being totally manipulated by Danny. He called from the hospital and wanted me to get him out. He had convinced the doctor that he wasn't a danger to himself or anyone else.

Against my better judgment I did.

But I knew—this could not go on.

Rehab #3: Third Time's A Charm

I PICKED UP DANNY from the hospital against my better judgment. I'm not quite sure at this point if I had any good "judgment" left. He wasn't very apologetic about his behavior and was actually angry at me for coming home the night before to check on him, and I think he blamed me for the situation he was in now, as usual.

I didn't care. I was not about to leave my children with a madman. Dr. Gary was now refusing to see Danny under any circumstances unless he checked himself into rehab. I was totally exhausted by his boorish behavior.

I needed a reprieve. Rehab sounded like what was best for him, not to mention our family. I couldn't keep Danny in the house with my kids. I knew this was horrible for them to witness. I backed Gary's call 100 percent. Danny had to go and get help. The production company found a rehab that would let them film.

Perfect! He would be forced to get help but also get his ego stroked by the whole thing being documented.

I drove with him to the place; he begged me not to make him check in for thirty days. I refused. He needed help and he was going to get it. I couldn't babysit him twenty-four hours a day. My children needed me, and they needed him, if he could ever get himself together.

I was growing tired of this vicious cycle of rehab, sobriety, falling-off-the-wagon routine. We drove in, and it was like a beautiful campground with cabins. I was seriously trying to figure out how I could rock a cocaine habit to check in for a thirty-day vacation myself.

As cushy as this sounds, it was putting Danny's radio show and our main source of income in serious jeopardy. Star 98.7 was in the middle of a book when Danny checked into rehab. This was going to prove problematic in the future.

Radio stations sell advertising by their book ratings. It is extremely important that during a book you are on your toes. Just like sweeps on TV, all hands are needed on deck. You had better be at the top of your game.

I would have thought having a member of a morning show in rehab would have been a ratings bonanza. The rehab center did allow Danny to make morning calls into the station periodically, so we were hoping that if he was fucked up again with drugs, at least he was doing his part to boost the ratings.

This rehab center offered different "alternative" methods of treating people: equine therapy, flute therapy, climbing up a telephone pole on bungee cords while your partner spots you. I was eager to participate in rehab exercises with Danny. The day we did the telephone-pole exercise, I showed up excited to be part of his recovery. The gentleman guiding the course asked who wanted to go first. I quickly volunteered. They hooked me up to the safety rigging, and the guy asked, on a scale of one hundred, what percentage I felt Danny had my back.

I thought for a second and came up with 50 percent.

I glanced over at Danny and noticed a darkness come over his face. He couldn't believe I would say 50 percent. He started having this gigantic meltdown. How could this man who had done such horrible things to me not get that 50 percent was being kind?

Through our whole marriage, Danny always demanded that everyone of his colleagues respect me and consult me and pretty much forced them to deal with me regarding any important decision. Publically he insisted everyone else hold me and my opinions in high regard. Privately, obviously, he wasn't doing that at all. When I publically called him out during this exercise, he could not handle it.

I started climbing the pole; it was unstable and was shaking a lot. Not the easiest thing to climb, especially when your husband is standing beneath you swearing like Alec Baldwin being chased down by the paparazzi. I kept my concentration and kept climbing to the top.

When I was almost there, he yelled, "You think I have you fifty percent? Then I'll hold on to this rope only fifty percent." I was getting angrier by the second. When I got to the top of the pole, I was expected to jump off onto a trapeze. I was very scared, but I'd be damned if I wasn't going to get something out of this exercise other than a tongue-lashing from Danny.

I closed my eyes and jumped—I made it! By the time I came down from the pole, Danny was storming off. I followed him and sat down to speak to him.

He did not want to be in rehab and wanted to leave. There was no way I could support his leaving at that point. I wanted him to stay in and *try* to get something valuable out of it. Before he went into rehab, we had put a bid on another house. I felt the house we were in was at its top-dollar value, and I wanted to buy another one to fix up and sell in a few years. While he was there, it was my job to get us moved into the new place. So when he was complaining that I didn't write him any love letters or poems while he was there, I seriously could not have taken on one more thing. Getting kids to school, taking care of them, filming a show, going back and forth from his rehab in Malibu, and moving us was all I could manage.

I loved the new house and set out to finish it up, as it needed to be completed. It was an old house that a doctor had built in 1926. The woman we purchased it from had done most of the heavy work, but the downstairs needed to be completed. The downstairs had no floors, and there was a bar from a movie set from the 1930s (*Seven Seas*) that needed to be restored. I also wanted to surprise Danny and build a 1920s-style screening room in one of the areas. I recruited my friend Dr. Gadget to get together theater-tiered seating and a high-end projector. My friend Kyla McTaggart handmade blood-red curtains around the entire room. It was beautiful!

When Danny finally finished his thirty days, I went to pick him up. They had a very nice graduation ceremony for him. He said he was happy to be going home to a house where we had never had any fights. A real clean slate.

Danny immediately returned to Star 98.7 and was back in the groove with a clear head and a positive attitude about life. A few weeks after his return, he was called into the boss's office and given his walking papers. Going to rehab during a book had given Jamie all the ammunition she needed to finally drive Danny off "her" show.

I decided to start going back to church and hoped Danny could make some nice friends there. He also was militant about attending AA meetings. He started bringing some of his new AA friends around. Some of them I liked, some not so much.

One day he brought home these two strippers. I tried to be polite, but I wasn't sure what he was up to. They seemed like nice enough people, but I was not sure they were wise choices as friends for Danny for obvious reasons. One of them had dated one of the guys from the band KISS. A few years later, she and I would actually become friends. She was a good singer, and sometimes we were on the same bill at clubs. We went out to lunch on day, and she told me that Danny had gone over to her house and kept trying to have sex with her. Fucking Danny! So you see, guys: rehab, AA, church—none of it mattered. If he could get away with something, he would still give it a try.

WORST DRESSED AT THE EMMYS, FALL 2005 OR 2006

WITH THE POPULARITY OF our VH1 show, we were able to score tickets to the Emmys in 2005. I had always wanted to go to the Emmys or the Oscars, and I was excited to finally get the chance. The biggest problem: what to wear.

I certainly did not want to show up in the same outfit as someone else.

My solution: make my own dress. I had found a seamstress in the barrio of downtown LA who would hand-make couture gowns for $250. Almost every red-carpet gown you saw me in during this time period was a gown that I'd designed and had made by this woman.

I noticed that the only people ever nominated for best dressed were nominees. Since our show was not nominated (there was no Emmy category for biggest douchebag to his wife on TV that year), I knew there was no chance I could be on the best-dressed list.

So I decided to take a shot at getting on the worst list, just for the extra publicity.

I found this plaid green-and-purple material that I knew was going to be risky for a long gown. I bought this velvet green material to make a bustle. If I had been starring in *Gone with the Wind*, this dress might have been a hit. We cut the material to be formfitting on top and fishtailed at the bottom. Had I picked black material or anything but plaid, it probably would have been beautiful.

The car picked us up to drop us at the Emmy location at the Shrine Auditorium. I have never loved doing red carpets and was working hard not to have a panic attack as we made it to the drop-off.

As we exited the car, fans started screaming and lights were flashing left and right. I held tight to Danny's arm as we walked through a gauntlet of photographers. People were yelling down from the audience how pretty they thought my gown was.

We made our way into the auditorium and took our seats. So many stars in one room!

I saw Tina Fey and Amy Poehler and tried to catch their eye, as I am a big fan. Amy and Tina did not wish to make friends with me. People think being at the awards is fun, and I am sure when you are a nominee it can be. Otherwise, you are pretty much trapped in your seat until the broadcast is over. It's waaaaaay overrated in my book, I'll watch at home with my wine and cheese and use the bathroom at will going forward.

The next week I went to band rehearsal with the Mudflapps and they were all acting rather odd. Finally, Chris Doohan, barely stifling a giggle, pulled out a copy a glossy magazine and said, "Uh, did you know about this?"

Right there on the Worst Dressed at the Emmy Awards page were me and Danny, front and center. I broke into an uncontrollable fit of laughter. I had tricked the Emmy fashion police into naming me worst dressed on purpose!

Gretchen Bonaduce: 1. Fashion Police: 0.

BREAKING BONADUCE SEASON TWO
OR AS FOR ME AND MY HOUSE
WE SHALL SERVE UP THE CRAZY

2006

WHEN THE RATINGS CAME in for season one, they were good enough to get us a season two. *The New York Times* wrote an article asking if reality TV had gone too far with *Breaking Bonaduce*. It shook some people up, for sure. People were used to hearing Ozzy say the F word in a funny context, not verbally abusing his wife with it.

A reporter from *Daily Variety* wrote that the "stench from *Breaking Bonaduce* was so bad you would need a lot of soap to wash it off." I was offended by this remark, so I decided to write him a note and send him a bar of soap to assist in helping get the stench of our show off.

I got a call from the VH1 press office a few days later asking if I had sent the reporter a bar of soap. I started laughing, thinking I was a genius! Our press agent was not amused and scolded me that I had made a very bad move.

Lucky for me, the reporter had a good sense of humor and wrote me back thanking me for the bar of soap, but wishing I had sent Jack Daniels instead. I wrote him back a note with a bunch of little airplane bottles of Jack and told him I felt he would be needing them for the next episodes.

We were hearing that Howard Stern was just talking and talking about how much he loved our show. I decided to send him a little package too. I wrote up a script with things to throw at the screen à la *Rocky Horror Picture Show*. I'm not sure if he got it, but my assistant Jaclyn Bradley and I had fun putting it together. Danny and I agreed we would spend season two repairing the damage to his reputation. This was going to be the feel good season!

Uuuuuuugghh! Not so fast.

For the first shooting dates, Danny was scheduled to travel down to Mexico City to meet with the actors who were going to be dubbing our voices in Spanish. He was supposed to be giving the actors direction on the tone of the show. And the scene they chose to show the actors was when the strippers showed up at my birthday party.

Danny had not watched any of the episodes, so this was the first time he had seen that episode. You could just see the rage starting to register on his face. He kepted yelling at the actor dubbing him in Spanish that he wasn't mad enough. And that was it. Season two was going to be every bit as volatile as season one.

Danny returned home, and from the second he walked through the door, he would not let the stripper thing go once again. You cannot move forward if you cannot let go of the past. I thought he was not sober, or clean, or at the minimum was possibly having a nervous breakdown. Danny's AA friends, at my request, tried to do an intervention on him because they thought something was up, too. Even Dr. Gary, during our first session for season two, was convinced that something was up with Danny.

Danny became so enraged by Dr. Gary challenging him on his sobriety that Danny fired Gary right there on the spot. I decided it was in all our best interest if Danny moved out for a while and got his own place. We found an apartment in Hollywood for him.

By 2006, I had been married to Danny for sixteen years. He couldn't fool me anymore. It wasn't going to work with me to just "wish" him sober and believe him when his behavior proved otherwise. The TV show producers, along with me and Gary, wanted proof to back up his claim. We all insisted that he take a urine test. I wanted him watched like a hawk because I already knew that he knew how to get around them.

Somehow Danny came back clean on his urine test. As I was writing this chapter, I decided to call the one person that had been around for the whole taping of the show. If my suspicions were correct, this person might have some insight as to how he could have come up clean on that urine test.

I was nervous to ask, but I needed to know for my own sake, and also so I could not be disputed in court if the subject came up. I said, "Do you know anything about how Danny came up clean on that test during the taping of the second season?"

They took a deep breath and said, "Yes, I know. I wanted to tell you for the longest time, so I am relieved that you are asking me. I took the test. I used the toilet before he went in. I peed in a plastic bag and left it in the bathroom." They added, "I did it for you and the kids. Danny said he would lose his job and everything if he came back with a positive result on the test. He said that he would not be able to take care of you and the kids, you would lose your house, and well, I just could not let that happen to you and the kids."

This person is one of the most stand-up, finest people I have ever known.

I knew the personal cost to them compromising their own integrity to save me and my children had weighed heavily on them. I just hated Danny for putting them in that position. Couldn't he just stay clean and not have to ask people to put themselves in that position?

UNCOUNSIOUS UNCOUPLING

2007

WHEN ALL WAS SAID and done, Danny and I were married a total of eighteen years to the day. I believe that Danny would have been dead or in jail without me, and if you look back on all the interviews that were done during our marriage, Danny said it himself many times. And I, most likely, would have amounted to very little myself without him. He made me want to be a better person. He spoke so highly of me that I didn't want to let him down. But the pedestal was too high for any mere human. I was bound to fall off.

When I look back and reflect on our time together, I do have to take some responsibility for the failure of our marriage. Maybe in some way I had caused a little of Danny's madness with my insistence that we keep our marriage together. Being so conditioned to work it out and stay together, ultimately I was forcing a very bad situation to continue. I loved Danny very much in the beginning, and we were very happy together for many years. One of Danny's family members and many of my friends agree with me that Danny's mental state started to deteriorate after his affair with 9021HO.

I think it ate at his mind to know that what he was doing was so wrong. Had he just told me he wanted a divorce before he went down the affair road, I could have lived with it. But sneaking around and moving her down the street, it would be over my dead body that that woman would be stepmother to my children.

I didn't want someone with the morals of Aleister Crowley, who lived by a *"Do what thou wilt shall be the whole of the Law"* kind of morality, to have any influence over my kids. Twelve years after the affair, at a concert with Dave Stewart and Ringo Starr in 2014, I felt a tap on my shoulder and turned around.

"Hi, Gretchen," she said. "Do you know who I am?" It took me a second to realize, and then she added, "I owe you an apology, and I was wondering if you would take my business card?"

I stuck my nose so far in the air and let her have it. Ten years of built up rage. She had to be thinking, no wonder Danny wanted away from her!

But I do give it up to her; she stood there and took it for about twenty minutes.

After unleashing all of that rage, I felt much better. I just felt sorry for her and had pity for her falling for Danny's line of crap.

Apparently her family and friends knew and were even sending them gifts! I guess when you come from a family with values like those, the apple doesn't fall far from the tree. I know my dad would have been on the first plane over with a bat beating my ass if he knew I was having an affair with a married man, not sending me scented candles and massage oils.

So, Danny, I do apologize to you for making you stay longer than you wanted. The person who dies with the most toys wins, and I think if you add it all up, we both won. Two wonderful kids, a sizable amount of money to split, a lot of great stories and memories. It was worth it. All worth it. At least to me. I can say that after all you put me and the kids through that I would do it all again (though I don't know if I would put the kids through that again). I hope that maybe in some way you have grown up and learned from your mistakes and now see how it's much easier to live a life of truth. It really does make life easier to live when you don't have to keep track of all the lies that you have to tell. It takes more lies to cover the first lies and becomes such a mangled, tangled web. Hopefully over the years you have had time to read this really good book. It's called the Bible. It has this list of ten things that are good advice. Ten rules to live by that would have made your life so much better.

But who am I to judge, right?

WHEN IN PARIS, ASK WHAT *KIND* OF COOL BAR

October 2008

MY DIVORCE HAD BEEN dragging on for almost two years. Primarily I would not sign because when I was served with my divorce papers I found out that Danny had sold a TV show without my knowledge—one that I was a producer on! When the show was filming in Australia, Danny lied to me and said he was going there to do stand-up. He knew what he was doing was wrong, or he would not have lied about it.

Neither our agent, nor Danny, nor the production company thought it was important to let me know that. Now that I was a single mother, I needed all the income I could get, and even more importantly, that producer credit could really help me and the kids. In this town, you're only as good as your last job.

To add insult to injury, it was an idea that I had come up with: "I Know My Kid's the Next Child Star." We brought this show to the table in exchange for not doing a third season of *Breaking Bonaduce* because Danny and I felt it would ruin our marriage. Since we ended up getting a divorce anyway, I regret that we did not do it. The income would have been helpful to both of us.

I was livid and told him that until he made that right with me (telling the production company to give me my title and measly producer fee), I would refuse to sign the divorce paperwork.

The show was an unmitigated disaster in Australia and was canceled after the first season. Apparently Aussies could not wrap their heads around adults being rude and cruel to children trying to get into showbiz.

At that point, I sanctimoniously signed the papers. Like all things that are done with malice, it usually blows up in your face. It looked like my divorce would be granted around the last week of October. And I thought to myself: This would be a great time to have a new adventure.

When I need an adventure, I call my international travel buddy, Angela Stulley. I had met Angela on a deep-sea dive in Barbados many years before. Danny and I were both certified divers and had quite a few dives under our belts. Danny and I found a deep-sea wreck dive that we wanted to go on. We had never been on a dive this deep before—each hemisphere you go down can make a dive a little bit more dangerous. The maximum depth on this dive was 150 feet, and Angela and her boyfriend at the time happened to be on the same dive. She was tall, blonde, beautiful, and had a knockout body, and I figured I had better make friends with her before Danny started flirting with her.

The deeper you go down, the faster you use up your air. Danny had not been paying attention to how much air was left in his tank, and didn't realize he didn't have enough air to ascend to the surface. You have to come up slowly from this depth, making safety stops along the way to prevent decompression illness. Because the air is compressed, you are breathing more of it, which means you are taking in more nitrogen. The body can only cope with so many bubbles in the blood, so the ascent must be slow.

Your final stop is usually fifteen feet for three minutes down to avoid getting the bends. He found me and motioned that he was running low on air, so we started to make our way to the surface. We had gone up about thirty feet when Danny's tank ran out of air. We were waaaaay too far down to just go to the surface and the last thing you want to do is panic. Now I have the only air, but before I give him my reserve, I have to make sure he isn't freaking out and capable of drowning us both. He is cool as a cucumber. I should have known...my husband thrived on risky behavior. I shoved my reserve in his mouth, and we safely made our way to the surface. Luckily I had enough air for both of us. Had I remembered how he was leering like a pervert at Angela, I might not have been so generous with my air supply!

I digress. Back to Angela.

I tell Angela that I am so up for a new adventure to start the next chapter of my life and we decide to go to Paris. I had never been there and it seemed like a good way to signify my new beginning as a single divorcée.

I flew to NYC and met up with Ang. Angela is like a world international traveler and has about a million miles on American Airlines. She generously loaned me miles so we could fly together business class to Charles de Gaulle. Of all the good fortune: the pilot recognized me and rolled out the red carpet for us! (I love my life.) We boarded first and made ourselves all cozy in our business/first-class seats. The flight attendants walked by with mimosas for the business/first-class passengers. Right as I was about to finish my first mimosa, the captain's voice came on over the speaker and said there was a problem with the aircraft and we would need to get off the plane and wait for another plane.

Boooooooo.

But then something magical happened. They had poured mimosas for the first-class cabin that they would need to throw away. Instead, they offered to give them to Angela and me.

Yay!!!!

As we exited the plane, the pilot let me and Angela sit in the cockpit and pretend to drive the plane! Mr. Pilot, wherever you are, I will always think fondly of you for putting your job on the line for the amusement of Ang and me!

We landed in Paris and took a cab to our hotel. It turned out that Angela was very ill with bronchitis. Any other friend would have surely cancelled on me. She informed me that she was so ill that we could do either day things or night. She is not capable of doing both.

I picked the night, which left me to my own devices during the day. I decided I would walk through the Place de la Concorde and go to the Louvre Museum. It was a beautiful day, but it looked as though it were going to rain. I stood in an impossibly long line to get inside the museum, something I am usually against doing, but this was the Louvre! I was so excited to see the wonderful art and was of course shocked at the tiny size of the *Mona Lisa*.

I started walking back to the hotel and became incredibly lost. I didn't know where I was and I spoke very little French.

A car full of guys pulled over and asked if I wanted to go somewhere.

I didn't. But they were kind enough to point me in the right direction of my hotel. I was so relieved when I walked through our hotel door.

It dawned on me that I had never ever been to a foreign country by myself. This was exactly what I needed. I had braved a country on my own, and Angela and I decided to celebrate my newfound confidence with drinks at the Hotel Coste. It was a trendy place and people had gathered from all over the world: Tanzania, Germany, Belgium. A very interesting crowd, indeed, and we settled in with the group quite nicely. One of the guys, Christoph, offered to become our unofficial tour guide. Or at least I think that was his name. (Hey, there was lots and lots of champagne on that trip.) After a few hours, the European group wanted to know if we would like to go with them to a great club!

Great club? We were in.

My first big lesson in going with strangers would be: Ask what kind of club. Which we didn't.

We jumped into a cab and drove to this great club, and I'll give you one guess as to what kind of club.

Yup, this was the second time in Europe I'd be going to a sex club against my will. Le Chandelle. Thank God it was divided into a bar section and a sex club section. Bet you can guess which side I did not go into, much to the chagrin of the annoying female pole dancer who'd been trying to get me to do otherwise.

The upside of the adventure was that we got invited to a secret masquerade ball. Our new friend Christophe, whom we had met earlier in the evening at Hotel Coste, invited us for the following night. Neither of us had anything to wear, or so I thought; Angela, my fashion-forward friend, actually had brought plenty of things she could have worn.

I was completely ambivalent about spending money on a very expensive dress, but then, when would I ever get invited to a secret masquerade ball in Paris again? I bought a beautiful purple silk dress and shoes. Christophe provided us with hot masks to wear. Angela had an ornate one and I opted for the sexy plain Batman style. We had the time of our lives and capped off the evening at a bar in the shadow of the Eiffel Tower. As we walked back to our hotel, Christophe leaned over and kissed me. The first man I had kissed since Danny. Can't beat that.

Thank you, God! Thank you for sending a cute European guy to kiss me in the twilight in Paris.

IT WAS LIKE 9 1/2 WEEKS,
ONLY IN EUROPE

October 2008

I LOVED SINGING WITH the Mudflapps, but they played out only once or twice a year. I wanted to play out a few times a month. They'd never be able to do that due to conflicting schedules. I called the Mudflapps the world's richest garage band. Almost everyone in the band was either a CEO of a company or working in incredibly lucrative fields. Too many Aspen or Hawaii trips to plan around.

So I decided to form my own band.

I'd gone with my friend Denise to see the eighties band Gene Loves Jezebel and saw the opening act: The Peppermint Creeps. They were fun and great musicians, so I asked them if they wanted to have a side project with me.

To my surprise, they agreed.

An incredibly talented bunch, the band included Tracy Michaels on drums, Macy Malone on guitar, and Billy Blade on bass. Macy recruited a keyboard player from a David Bowie tribute band, Beth Corrigan. I wanted to form an eighties tribute band because I'm old. Well, getting that way. I thought that since I had sung those songs for so long, the lyrics would be the easiest for me to remember.

Next, we needed a name.

I'd been watching the History Channel and saw a TV program about Ankhesenamen, King Tut's wife. I thought that would be an incredibly cool name for our band, not factoring in that nobody could pronounce it or even remember it, for that matter. A boneheaded move on my part. Most people thought we were a progressive jazz band or heavy metal because of the name. We started rehearsals, and immediately I noticed that Tracy Michaels was late a lot. He was one of those rare musicians that were so great that you would put up with almost any behavior as long as you got to play with them.

I didn't realize he was ill.

He was so good that he would constantly upstage me with his antics behind me on the drums. Some people would be very pissed off about that, but I loved it. He totally made me up my game.

After about five months of rehearsals, The Peppermint Creeps decided to go on a short US tour. We would need to put Ankh on hiatus for a few weeks. While playing a date in Texas, the band all piled into one hotel room to save money. The next morning when they woke up, they noticed that Tracy wasn't breathing. He had rolled off the bed and was lying on the floor. They desperately tried to give him CPR, but they couldn't bring him back.

My daughter, Isabella, took this news especially hard. I think she's always felt a bit outside of the norm, and when I introduced her to The Peppermint Creeps, she found a group she could relate to. They were always incredibly kind to her and invited her to their gatherings.

They held Tracy's funeral at the Hollywood Forever Cemetery. Every Goth-looking, hair-metal-band person in Los Angeles showed up. It was a beautiful ceremony, and everyone could see how loved and respected Tracy was. His wife and best friend decided to put on a benefit concert to pay for funeral expenses and hopefully have some money left over to give to his children. We had six drummers sitting in with our particular band to play songs that we played with Tracy.

It was a wonderful evening except for the constant band drama. Geez. Let me tell you guys, people in bands in Los Angeles have such unbelievable egos.

One of the drummers that filled in, Ringo (just a nickname, I promise) was about 6'4" with a black rock-and-roll haircut, a great body, and a big nose (which I am a total sucker for; Adrian Brody's nose is my holy grail). This guy was hot!

We took a vote and all decided that Ringo (again, not his real name) was the person that Tracy Michaels would be most happy to have replace him in the band if he would have had a say. Ringo agreed to join.

I also decided to add another girl to the band. I think a violin player adds class to anything you're doing, and so I invited Alyson Montez to join the line up as well. As far as I knew, there were no eighties bands with a violin and thought it would give us an advantage.

We started rehearsals once again, and Macy quit. Crap.

I didn't realize that this was the Hollywood band life. People are in and out all the time. Lucky for me, Beth was married to a guy that seemed interested in taking Macy's place. I was so relieved that I would not have to audition people for the spot. Good guitar player, good voice, very nice dude. He'd do.

Now I know you are going to think I'm making this up.

I'm not.

Two years in, Bernie was in a horrible freak accident and passed away as well, and I was starting to wonder if being in a band with me is dangerous to your health. Two incredible musicians and people, both dead, both in my band. I can't even think of any huge bands that have had that kind of bad luck.

We received an offer to play the after-party at the "Really Awards" reality show at the Avalon. Ringo informed me that I should announce that he was single, which was news to me. In between one of the sets, I said, "Hey, everybody, my drummer is single," and all these girls make a beeline to Ringo. (If this were the real Ringo, I'm sure this would have also held true.) At the end of the evening, Ringo lets me know that actually that information was for me. Do you know what the number one rule in a band is? Don't date someone in your band.

So, what do I do? Of course I accept a date with him.

A few nights later, we played a lesbian bar in West Hollywood and at the end of the evening, Ringo kissed me.

Total fireworks! Oh boy. I was in trouble now.

We went on a wonderful date and within a week I was head over heels for this man.

I quickly made an appointment at my OB/GYN, because obviously we were going to be in a relationship and I needed to figure out my birth control method. In the almost two years since Danny and I broke up, I hadn't been with a man sexually.

My doctor ran my blood levels and informed me that my hormone levels were so low that I would have to be aggressive about hormone therapy if I ever wanted to have another child. What I heard was: You can't get pregnant anymore. Yay for me! I was a pretty heavy smoker at the time and so the pill was absolutely out of the question for me, so this was unbelievably welcome news.

When Ringo and I first started dating, he was also in a fantastic band called the Lords of Altamont. They were planning a summer tour through France and Italy, and luckily for me, they allowed me to join them at the end of the tour. I jumped on the plane by myself, at this point an old pro after Paris with Angela. I flew into Rome and hired a car to drive me to the village.

Unfortunately, at the last minute, the hotel they were supposed to be staying at had changed. I was planning on meeting up with Ringo at the hotel. This was going to be problematic. Somehow, without speaking a word of Italian, I was able to track him down at a street festival a few villages away from my hotel.

I was so happy to be back in his arms after four weeks. That evening, in our little romantic hotel, we made passionate crazy love. We sat in the front of the van as we drove through Italy making out as we passed sunflower fields across Italy.

That would be the theme for the entire trip. We would drive all day to the Lords' show, and then afterward we would go back to the hotel and make love almost all night till we were exhausted. I was so incredibly in love (lust) with this man and I was in Europe having crazy sex in monasteries, in hostels. It was *nine and a half* weeks—only in Europe!

Once we returned home, Ankhesenamen had a gig at a festival in Lake Arrowhead. I wasn't feeling too well so I decided just out on a whim to take a pregnancy test. Of course, my body had betrayed me. I had done my due diligence and thought that I didn't need to worry about that. That's how incredible passion for somebody can override scientifically what your body should or should not be capable of doing.

What was I going to do? I was forty-three, on medication that was not approved for women who were pregnant, and not at all in a position where Ringo could possibly marry me. Definitely the worst rock and a hard place I have ever found myself in. Every year after the age of thirty-five, the chances of having a child with Down syndrome go up dramatically. I also didn't think Danny's alimony should be used to take care of another man's child. I sat down and talked to Ringo about it.

Luckily, I was only a few weeks along and they had a pill so that I wouldn't have to endure an abortion, which I don't even think I could've ever done. Under different circumstances, both Ringo and I would have definitely wanted to have the baby. I think about it often, and I know he does as well. It was definitely a testament to our incredible love for one another that we conceived a child when I should not have been able to.

But the reality was, the timing was all wrong.

MON CHERIE

WHEN I FIRST PUT together a band, my intention was to play casinos or high-paying festival gigs. I was basically clueless about how hard it was to get good-paying gigs in Los Angeles. Many of the bars here are pay to play, which means you have to guarantee that you will sell a certain amount of tickets by paying the venue that money before you even step on stage. Many times I would get stuck eating tickets that I had to buy up front and couldn't unload. On top of that, drawing a large crowd in LA is difficult. There are just are so many choices for entertainment.

One weekend, we played a street festival in Los Feliz, a cool little enclave not far from Hollywood. They were going to be providing backline, which meant the venue would supply the speakers, drum kit, mikes, and PA—all the band had to do is show up with our instruments.

This should have been my first clue that we were on the verge of disaster.

Musicians don't loan out their best stuff for a charity event or street fair. Instead, the venue gets the stuff they don't care about, which is why using provided backline might blow up in your face. Sure, there's a lot less for load in/out, but it's not worth the risk of catastrophic equipment failure.

Of all the gigs in the world, of course, who would turn up to this one?

Ohhhh, only my rock-goddess idol: Cherie Currie, lead singer of the first creditable all-girl rock-and-roll band, the Runaways. She had seen me on *Dr. Phil* recently and the appearance had piqued her interest in an introduction. Our mutual friend, Ron, had talked her into coming out to see us play live. He had talked Ankh up so much. I mean, how could she not want to come out and see my middle-aged ass crushed into a Madonna bustier?

I should have known the second my bass player Billy plugged his amp into the backline bass cabinet and it started to smoke that this gig was not going to be our finest hour. We stepped on the stage and my violin player started the first notes of "Kids in America." For some reason, she was horribly out of tune. The people in the audience looked as though they were being physically injured by the sound coming off the stage.

Trying to mix sound when you are playing outside is very difficult. I could tell the sound guys were struggling to dial it in and it was one of those situations where the show must go on—even if you knew the "show" was sounding like dog shit.

Near the end of our set, the backline drum decided to give up the ghost as well. Each song Ringo played, he noticed the drum coming a little more apart. By the last song he was chasing the bass drum across the stage in an effort to continue to play. It's the first time I've ever witnessed a drummer walking and playing a stationary drum! By the last note, Ringo had dropkicked the bass drum into the crowd.

Why, God, why? Of all the gigs, why did Cherie have to be at this one?

As I exited the stage, head hung low, I saw her and Ron sitting outside of a cafe. Lucky for me, she knew Ron would not have dragged her forty miles to see a band *this* bad. She regaled me with stories of bad Runaway gigs and made me feel better. From that point on we've practically been sisters.

GIMMIE MY REALITY SHOW

August 2008

AFTER DANNY AND I divorced, I wasn't sure I would be able to work in showbiz again. But here is where you reap what you sow. I had cultivated so many great relationships; people were still totally willing to help me out. AND I had a guardian angel: Ms. Laurie Muslow. One thing you have to know about Hollywood is this: Your Hollywood friends are not your real friends. You had better never mistake that fact. Laurie was one of the few exceptions to the rule. Every job I have ever gotten out here after Danny, she was responsible for getting it for me. Laurie called me and asked me if I would be interested in going out for this show called *Give Me My Reality Show*. It was a job, and it paid. Of course I was.

I met up with Natural Nine productions and they asked me questions and put the interview on tape. I had just played Gay Pride the day before, so I still had my funky Native American hairdo. (I had been channeling one of the Village people.) Natural Nine had produced the Really Awards a few months back where Danny threw Johnny Fairplay on the ground during the broadcast. I felt a little awkward with them as I was pretty horrified that Danny would do such a thing. (We were already in the works for our divorce, so he had attended with his girlfriend, Amy.) We spoke about it a little bit, and I went about my business. A few days later I learned I had been chosen to be in the cast. I was so excited to be working and bringing in a paycheck.

The cast would include me, Susan Olsen, Traci Bingham, Kato Kaelin, Ryan Starr, A. J. Benza, and Bobby Trendy. George Gray was the host of the show, which was weird because he was in our pilot of

Rock and Roll Dinner Party. The concept was that contestants shoot their own reality show and America would vote. Whoever won got their own show.

I was pretty sure there was no way in hell that I could win, as I did not have an *American Idol* following or a *Baywatch* following, but I knew because I produced shows and was pretty good at it, I would deliver the best show and that would be good enough for me.

One of the competitions was to pick a producer out of a pool of thirty or so. Whoever won the challenge would pick first, then second place, and so on. There was a woman named Jen who immediately caught my eye, but AJ had grabbed her. We each got to pick four to interview and throw the other three back into the pot. AJ put her back into the pot, and I quickly grabbed her up for my own. I know she was secretly hoping to get Ryan or Traci. She didn't even know who I was. But Jen was going to work for me and she was going to love it! My idea for my show was basically to shoot my life. I had just started dating again (this was before Ringo and I hooked up), had started a clothing line, was a single mother, and had an eighties band.

I pretty much made an ass out of myself on TV as I was sure I couldn't win anyway. The reality awards taped on my birthday September 24, 2008, and the show launched right after the award show.

Somehow the last three contestants standing were me, Kato, and Traci. Backstage, I asked both of them if they would be upset if they didn't win. Both of them were so smug in their answers—they both thought they were going to win.

Kato said, "YES! Are you kidding, this is my shot!"

Since I had gotten to know Kato during the taping of this show, I felt sorry for him with all his bad showbiz breaks. Apparently he had been up for one of the main rolls in the movie *Dumb and Dumber*. The week they were going to announce the actor who had been cast, OJ decided to kill his wife. Because of all the negative publicity on the case, Kato believed he had lost the part because of it. I felt bad for him, and thought I'd be just as happy if he won and got a break.

I didn't give a rat's ass about Traci, because she wasn't a very nice person, and I was very disappointed at the shots she took at me when the show aired. They called me out from backstage first to reveal the results. They had a map of the United States and lit up each state that you took, mimicking the presidential election results.

The entire map lit up—I was the only person who got a vote in each state! I knew you only had to have one vote in a state for the state to light up, but it still seemed like a pretty good sign. And this was *entirely* thanks to MySpace and one of my new best friends, Cherie Currie. As mentioned earlier, Cherie, as the former lead singer of the Runaways, made it her personal job to get everyone she knew to vote over and over for me.

The next thing they said was that I had taken the majority of the states with the most votes. More than half of the map lit up. The audience went crazy!

This was exciting, yet it was starting to sink in that I was probably going to get my ass kicked and it was going to be embarrassing. I left the stage feeling ambivalent that the next time I took the stage, I would be voted off.

They brought out Traci and Kato and did the same map thing with them. And then finally they brought us all out together. As we stood on stage standing next to each other, they eliminated the first contestant. It was Kato! He flipped out and stormed off the stage and refused to come back on. Wow…I had never seen such bad sportsmanship in my life. Now I was GLAD he lost.

It was down to me and Traci. We held hands. I closed my eyes and waited for them to say her name, this was it! And the winner is *drum roll* Gretchen Bonaduce!

You should have seen my face. Better yet, you should have seen Traci's face. Utter shock, followed by horror, followed by thinly masking a happy face for me. I could not believe it, and neither could Traci. Apparently for the next week, she and her manager were on the phone with Natural Nine complaining that she had lost. Yes, Traci, you're right. They for sure wanted the person with the fewest votes to win.

Another sore loser. Geez, Hollywood people are such babies.

Ringo and I had just started dating, and he was in the audience, as were my parents, my friends, and my band members. It was such an amazing surprise. I started planning out story ideas for my show right away.

I had informed Ringo that part of the show I had won with was the idea of me dating. I wasn't sure how that would sit with him. I tried to let him off the hook and told him if he wanted to postpone getting serious with me, I would understand, but I was committed to do the show I had won with. He said he could handle it, as he was going to be one of the guys I was dating either way, since we were going out.

After my divorce was final, one of the guys that had asked me out was Danny's divorce attorney. Isn't that hilarious? I wanted to go out with him because I am sure a divorce attorney hears all the worst things about you, so I was intrigued as to why he wanted to take me out to dinner. I thought it would make for a great segment on my show.

The producers had put a profile of me up on a few dating sites so that we would have a few guys to choose from. The one thing I did not want to do was be unkind to some poor guy on TV that thought it would be a kick in the pants to take me out on a date. All of the guys that they fixed me up with were extremely nice people. The producers wanted me to pick one of them to go out with again. I picked a gentleman who was an archaeologist. His particular area of expertise was the study of dead languages. Fascinating guy! We decided our second date would take place at a dog park in the Hollywood Hills. He showed up for our date with a big metal Ankh symbol because he knew that was the name of my band. Cute!

We sat on a bench and we talked about the end of the world that was projected to be December 21, 2012. He promised me that we would not need to worry about that date. He said the end of the world would come via aliens.

As we sat there on the bench, two dogs came running to where we were seated and decided to start humping on top of my feet. We could not have paid for that to happen in real life. So funny! Ultimately, I was falling for Ringo so I was glad when the dating part of my show was over.

I also was covering my clothing line, band, and just being a single mother. I think my ratings were pretty good (not like Kardashian good), but unfortunately the network went under when I was waiting to hear if I would be getting a second season.

I'm not sure if the outside world understands how hard it is to get a show on TV. As of this writing, I have done many guest spots, but my own show has eluded me. It would be great to get one more on-camera show, just so I can try to get considered for *Dancing with the Stars* or *Celebrity Apprentice*, but otherwise I prefer being behind the camera these days. Maybe one of these days I'll get a lucky break again. But how many lucky breaks can one expect in life?

CAN I PLEASE HAVE AN
IN-SHAPE STALKER

Here's a downside of putting up flyers for your band in your own neighborhood: attracting the wrong attention—the kind that might follow you home! My grocery store was supportive of local talent and would allow me to post pictures and info about upcoming dates for my band. Whenever I had a show, the manager at Albertson's would allow me to put up flyers for the event.

One day I pulled into my driveway and jumped out of my car with several bags full of groceries. My driveway was quite steep, and so many times as you drove up the tires would squeal loudly.

As I walked to the back door, I heard tires squealing wildly behind me.

I turned around and saw a heavyset, Sasquatch-looking female driving up the driveway. My boyfriend, Ringo, heard the commotion outside and came out to see what the trouble was. I couldn't hear exactly what she was saying…but I heard Ringo angrily yelling at her to get off my property.

As I turned around to approach her car, I could finally hear what she was yelling: "This is my house, and you're trespassing. I work for the CIA and I will have them come here and shoot all of you for trespassing on my property if you don't leave!"

I calmly looked at her and said, "Lady, this is my house—not yours."

She yelled back, "Who's on the title??? Who's on the title? That's right! It's Gretchen Bonaduce, and that's me!"

My house assistant at this point had come out to see what was going on as well and was trying to reason with the insane Sasquatch in her broken English. "No, Ma'am, this not your house, this is her house," she said, motioning at me.

This nut was going apeshit insisting that my house was hers!

After the "I will send the CIA to kill you all" comment, I decided it was probably a good idea to call 911.

In the meantime, Ringo had lost his patience with Looney Tune and was demanding she leave the property. As she backed up, almost into the street, Ringo thought fast and pulled her keys out of the car and threw them into the bushes across the street to try to delay her until the police showed up. This, of course, forced her to get out of the car to try to fish for her keys in the bushes. But first she turned her wrath on Ringo and started attacking him. Mind you, Ringo is a 6'5" guy, so that takes quite a lot of balls to come after a guy that size.

Now, it dawns on me that this lady had likely been running around telling people she was me! I could hear the conversations that must have followed. *"Wow, have you seen Gretchen Bonaduce? Since her divorce from Danny, she has really gone downhill!"*

The next day I receive a text from Danny's new wife, Amy.

She says, "Uh…did you know there is someone on Twitter that says she is you, Twiggy Ramirez, and Charles Manson?"

"Uh, yeah," I informed her. "She just came over to say hello, actually."

Even Danny, who could give a rat's ass about me, was concerned enough to give me the heads up. Luckily for me, she was already on the police radar for her erratic behavior. I think she was very mentally ill, and I was able to get a restraining order against her. I'm not sure if she had been following me for a while, or if she had seen my name on the flyer, recognized me at the grocery store, and gone home to Google me on her computer and somehow figured out where I lived. She lived less than a mile away from me. It completely changed my life. I couldn't leave Dante at home by himself anymore. I was terrified she would show up when I wasn't there. Not sure what ever happened to her, but I was certainly glad to move out of my own house with my children to a new place so that she didn't know where I lived anymore.

YOU MEAN THE JOINT ACTUALLY MEANS A JOINT? I THOUGHT IT MEANT A COOL HANG OUT PLACE

ONE OF THE MANY wonderful DJs I met through Danny was a beautiful and smart woman named Sam Phillips—a former penthouse pet. Gorgeous and smart, so basically everything you could want to hate in a person!

She had me on her show *The Single Life* after Danny and I divorced to talk about being single and pursuing my musical career. I decided if I was going to get a chance to sing live on the radio, I had better bring in the big guns. I called Cherie Currie to see if she wanted to come in and sing too.

Cherie was up for it and called in another big gun, Yvette Barlow, from En Vogue. We decided to do the Runaways hit "Cherry Bomb," each of us taking a verse. Now, you have to understand, people, these were two very accomplished singers, and letting me sing was like letting the janitor at the recording studio step in and take a crack at things.

We had a fabulous time on the show and taught "Cherry Bomb" a thing or two.

Later, she had my band The Fatal '80s on her new radio show where we sang and played live. Her show at the time was called *Sam's Pajama Party*, and so we were all dressed in our jammies. (I had Elmo ones, a gift from drummer Troy Patrick Farrell from the band White Lion and his girlfriend at the time, Suzy.) The Fatal '80s lineup at this time included Ringo, Murv Douglas, Laura Saggers, and Matt Fuller—who usually toured in the group Puddle of Mudd.

We were drinking mimosas and basically acting like a fun rock band, and the management loved us so much they offered me my own show! I decided to recruit Murv as my cohost as he was a super good sport and didn't mind taking a totally ridiculous take on subjects if need be.

I called on all my friends to help write parody songs and ridiculous drops that we could use during the show. My friend Bill Morgan, who does voiceover work in NYC (and also owns the bar the Stonewall in NYC, where the famous riots in the sixties took place over gay rights), made some hilarious drops for our animal adoption segment, including, "Who wants Gretchen's soft, hairy pussy?" and, "This bitch needs a home!" for the female dogs.

We pulled stories that were crazy from the news, mostly from the *Huffington Post*, and tried to showcase an unsigned band each week. That went on for quite a few months until something happened that shut the place down. It took me until the last week of our show to figure out The Joint was being funded by a thing called Speed Weed, where they would drive your ganja to your house.

Sometimes I'm dense. The Joint? (I get it now!)

Once that went south, Sammy came to the rescue again and was able to get me and Murv a show on Film On in Beverly Hills. We tried to do the same show, but when you're dealing with, essentially, crack addicts and Internet trolls, there isn't a real opportunity to do a quality show. The worst part was putting our friends in unsigned bands in the position to be ridiculed. I cried after every show, horrified at the verbal trauma our friends were being put through.

Another case of God working in mysterious ways: eventually the owner of Film On decided to change directions, giving pretty much everyone their walking papers in the process.

I've never been so happy in my life to be let go of a job.

Sometimes, like a relationship, none is better than the one you have.

THINGS I HAVE LEARNED
IN MY FIFTY-TWO YEARS

IF YOU'RE GOING TO have a beer can stuck to your face after a beer bong, Budweiser is in a silver and red can. Looks good with everything.

An apple pie is a good choice if you need to pee on a pie.

If you're going to stalk me, please be in the 105 to 115 range.

There is no I in team.

Putting your kids on reality TV can completely blow up in your face.

Do not leave sewn-in extensions in your hair for thirteen years. You will pay in the long run. Just trust me on this one.

Sam-I-Am does not like green eggs and ham.

If you are not famous and have sex with a lot of famous guys, you're pretty much a groupie. (Or you also could be a Kardashian.) Same thing.

Don't sweat the small stuff. I had to many gigantic things to sweat over so the small stuff never got to me.

And above all, for God's sake…just have fun and make the most of your life! It's not just a saying, you really only do live once.

WHO LIVES, WHO DIES,
WHO TELLS YOUR STORY

Chicago, February 2018

THE PLACE TO END is in the place it all began fifty-two, almost fifty-three years ago: back home in Chicago. This time with my boy for his seventeenth birthday. I tried to think of a great way to celebrate his special day and decided to bring him to Chicago to see *Hamilton*. It was cheaper for me to fly to Chicago and buy two tickets than it was to buy one ticket in Los Angeles.

I cashed in some of my points to bring the Count first class, and we arrived late afternoon. My best guy friend of thirty years, Adam; my friend Barbara, whom I consider a second mother to my children; and her son and his girlfriend all smashed into a booth to enjoy some delicious pizza.

After dinner, Barb's son Kyle treated us to a show at Second City, where he is a manager. I wouldn't be surprised at all if we end up seeing half that cast on *Saturday Night Live* one day soon. It was so cold out as we walked back to Barb's car, but I was so happy to be able to wear my big faux furry hat. I'm a hat girl for sure. You can sometimes wear them in LA if the temperature drops enough, as long as you don't mind being ridiculed in sixty-five degrees.

I don't. I wear them anyway, but here was an opportunity to just blend into the crowd.

When we arrived at her house, we were pretty exhausted from the flight and dinner and decided to crawl right into bed. Barb's two-hundred-pound dog, Ben, decided that I was going to be the lucky sleeping buddy for the night. It turns out, not only do I make a duck face in all pictures on Facebook, I apparently make the same face in my sleep as evidenced by the sneaky picture Barb took of me and Ben curled up together on the bed. (I will get you one day, Barb—watch out where you fall asleep!)

The following day, we decided to rent a hotel downtown since our *Hamilton* tickets were for that evening and we could check in early and see some of the sights. We stayed at the Congress Hotel across the street from Lake Michigan. An older hotel built at the turn of the century, it's glory days were in the past, but I loved it. I love the Queen Mary in Long Beach almost as much. Just like people, I like things a little worse for wear. We walked over to the Field Museum. So many memories came flooding back. I told Barb and the Count how I had served as a PA on the original *Flatliners* with Julia Roberts and Kiefer Sutherland at the Field Museum. That job lasted one day, as I was way more concerned about making showbiz contacts than I was stopping people walking by when they were filming a shot. Such a loser. I remembered having coffee at the Artiste Café with my friend Steph and then doing a student photo shoot at Columbia University. So many good times.

For dinner we decided to eat at the Berghoff restaurant, as it was down the street from the theater where *Hamilton* was playing. My friends and I never ate there when we were starving roommates. We couldn't afford to. And I certainly could never have flown first class and complained about buying my own drinks! Times have changed. Yes, they have.

I had been trying to figure out a way to end this book and truly could not find the inspiration to do so until *Hamilton*.

We entered the theater and found our seats. I had been waiting for a year to see this Broadway show since I had seen the PBS special about it. It was so good, I almost started weeping. So original. The lyrics, the music, the actors and singers. The only other musical to affect me like that was *Jesus Christ Superstar*, and I'm pretty sure I am on their no-entry potential-stalker list as I have seen it so many times.

Then the character Eliza Hamilton went into the last number, "Who Lives, Who Dies, Who Tells Your Story." This was succinctly why I wanted to write this book. I wanted to tell my story. Thank you, Lin Manuel Miranda, for helping me try to explain to people why I wanted to do it.

I lived, I'm not dead yet, and I did get to tell my story. At least my story so far.

ACKNOWLEDGMENTS

To my parents Tom, Wanda, and Mary. Thank you for being my parents. The book I should have written is about what wonderful human beings you are. That would be a gigantic book. I'm sure after you read this one, you will wish instead I had written that as well! Seat belts, please.

To Kurt, Derek, and Aimee. Glad you're my siblings. Although we don't see each other or speak often, I'm still very glad we share DNA.

Kevin. My handyman. The fixer of all things including my heart. I love you.

To Hixson High School. Thank you for letting me be second in all things. Second most votes for funniest, second in the talent contest. Coming in second did not usually get your picture in the yearbook. Thank you for helping me keep my awkward and chubby adolescent pictures to a minimum in the universe.

To Barbara Olson, Angela Stulley, Yvette Klobachar, Adam Becvaree, and to Mary for not punching me in the face when I leaned to hard on AB. My 20plus club. Lots and lots of shenanigans have been had over the twenty-odd years. I love you guys to the moon and back.

To my Broodie sisters. Cherie Currie, Pam Apostolou, Leslie Koch Froumburg, Paula Tricky, Jeanne Russell, Sheena Metal (Jenny), Susan Olsen. Nothing but love.

To Adrianne Curry. Man, have we moved each other a few times or what? You are my Midwest girl touchstone. Glad we had each other to not let our heads get too big. But if you had a bigger head, just more room for that gorgeous face!

Alyssa Crosby my BFF (that's a hard job to keep), Pol Atteu, Patrik Simpson, Shelly Pine Freidman, Michael Von London, Jackie Kallen, Marie Currie, Stephanie Mandel, Laurie D. Muslow, always and forever my LA Tribe. (Even though some of you have moved away.)

To the amazing Doc Michelle Ware from the Los Feliz Med Spa. I showed you my old driver's license. You know what you've done! They say money can't buy happiness. Cool scupting and botox can, though!

To Tricia O'Gorman and Idalia Guadamuz. My sanity and saviors on too many occasions to count.

Jaclyn Bradley Palmer. One of the finest humans I know. You were always more to me than our assistant. I entrusted everything important to me to you. My children, my secrets, my heartache. And I knew it was all in good hands.

To Ankh, The Fatal '80s, The Mudlaps, Gay C/DC for letting me sing back up for you. Macy, Billy, Alyson, Beth, Bernie, Murv, Ringo, Laura, Walter, Don E., Edward, Bob, and Matt and Crystal. Thanks for playing with me.

To this guy, Joe Di Prisco, for this little exchange:

Subject: RE: Tyson from Rarebird told me to reach out. Gretchen Bonaduce here

Dear Gretchen,

Tyson is easily the best publisher I have worked with—and I've published lots of books with other houses. He is very talented, very smart, very connected, and very reliable.

Just so you know, these are not adjectives that I would use for many people in the book business.

I'll go one step further: I trust him.

Happy to discuss with you, or to answer any specific questions you may have.

In the meantime, best of luck to you in your fascinating career—and with your book.

Ciao,

Joe

ME:

Hey Joe! Thank you.

Tyson seems to be all of those things, which is quite flattering that someone who all those adjectives apply to would be interested in my little ol' book.

The word trust and a man are not words I usually use in the same sentence. Hahaha.

I also very much appreciate your assessment of my career being fascinating BTW.

According to Wikipedia I am an "excuse maker and an enabler" so I am going to set that shit straight right now that I am actually "fascinating!"

Big question... Did you make money??

You are awesome for taking the time to answer.

Best.

GB

Which of course brings me to Rarebird. Thank you Tyson, Alice, Julia, Guy (who I am sick of), Gregory, Jake, and Hailie. BIG thank you to all the publishers who passed so I ended up here. Thank you Natalie O'Bando for your hand in this.

To Danny, I can honestly say this book would not be possible without you. Thank you for being the father of our two amazing and wonderful children.

And lastly, thank you Two Buck Chuck. You definitely weren't the least.